Phonics and Sight Words

This book belongs to:

CONTENTS:

Letter A ....**Page 1**
Sight Word "and" ....Page 5
Sight Word "a" ....Page 6
Sight Word "as" ....Page 7
Sight Word "are" ....Page 8
Letter M ....**Page 9**
Sight Word "my" ....Page 13
Sight Word "many" ....Page 14
Sight Word "more" ....Page 15
Sight Word "make" ....Page 16
Letter T ....**Page 17**
Sight Word "to" ....Page 21
Sight Word "two" ....Page 22
Sight Word "the" ....Page 23
Sight Word "this" ....Page 24
Letter S ....**Page 25**
Sight Word "see" ....Page 29
..Sight Word "she" ....Page 30
Sight Word "so" ....Page 31
Sight Word "some" ....Page 32
..**Letter I** ....**Page 33**
Sight Word "I" ....Page 37
Sight Word "is" ....Page 38
Sight Word "into" ....Page 39
Sight Word "it" ....Page 40
Letter F ....**Page 41**
Sight Word "find" ....Page 45
Sight Word "for" ....Page 46
Sight Word "from" ....Page 47
Sight Word "first" ....Page 48
Letter D ....**Page 49**
Sight Word "do" ....Page 53
Sight Word "did" ....Page 54
Sight Word "day" ....Page 55
Sight Word "down" ....Page 56
Letter R ....**Page 57**
Sight Word "run" ....Page 61
Sight Word "ride" ....Page 62
Letter O ....**Page 63**
Sight Word "on" ....Page 67
Sight Word "of" ....Page 68
Sight Word "out" ....Page 69
Sight Word "over" ....Page 70
Letter G ....**Page 71**
Sight Word "go" ....Page 75
Sight Word "get" ....Page 76
Sight Word "good" ....Page 77
Sight Word "green" ....Page 78
Letter L ....**Page 79**
Sight Word "like" ....Page 83
Sight Word "look" ....Page 84
Sight Word "long" ....Page 85
Sight Word "little" ....Page 86
Letter H ....**Page 87**
Sight Word "he" ....Page 91

Sight Word "here" .... Page 92
Sight Word "have" .... Page 93
Sight Word "how" .... Page 94
Letter U .... **Page 91**
Sight Word "use" .... Page 99
Sight Word "up" .... Page 100
Letter C .... **Page 101**
Sight Word "can" .... Page 105
Sight Word "come" .... Page 106
Sight Word "call" .... Page 107
Sight Word "could" .... Page 108
Letter B .... **Page 109**
Sight Word "be" .... Page 113
Sight Word "big" .... Page 114
Sight Word "before" .... Page 115
Sight Word "by" .... Page 116
Letter N .... **Page 117**
Sight Word "no" .... Page 121
Sight Word "now" .... Page 122
Sight Word "not" .... Page 123
Sight Word "number" .... Page 124
Letter K .... **Page 125**
Review beginning sound .... Page 129
Review beginning sound .... Page 130
Letter V .... **Page 131**
Review beginning sound .... Page 135
Review beginning sound .... Page 136
Letter E .... **Page 137**
Sight Word "each" .... Page 141
Word search .... Page 142
Letter W .... **Page 143**
Sight Word "write" .... Page 147
Sight Word "we" .... Page 148
Sight Word "was" .... Page 149
Sight Word "what" .... Page 150
Sight Word "when" .... Page 151
Sight Word "word" .... Page 152
Letter J .... **Page 153**
Sight Word "just" .... Page 157
Sound short "a" .... Page 158
Letter P .... **Page 159**
Sound short "e" .... Page 163
Letter Y .... **Page 165**
Sight Word "yes" .... Page 169
Sight Word "you" .... Page 170
Sight Word "yellow" .... Page 171
Sight Word "your" .... Page 172
Letter X .... **Page 173**
Sound short "i" .... Page 175
Letter Q .... **Page 177**
Sound short "o" .... Page 181
Letter Z .... **Page 183**
Sound short "u" .... Page 187
Answer key .... **Page 189**

LETTER A

Trace the letter **A**:

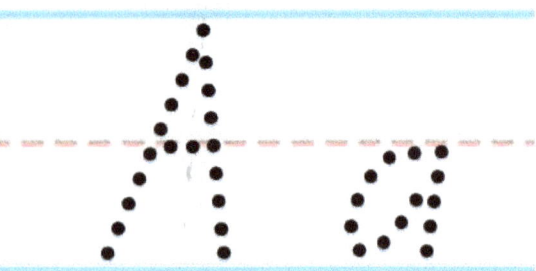

Write an upper and lower case letter **A**:

- Color all the items that begin with the **A** sound:

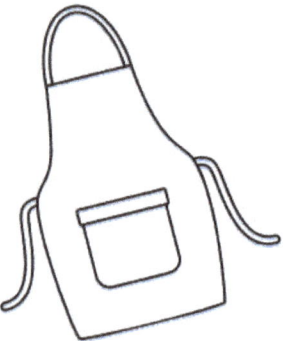

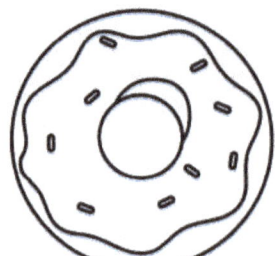

LETTER A

- Say the name of each picture. Circle each picture that begins with the **a** sound.

LETTER A

- Color only the squares with letter **A**.

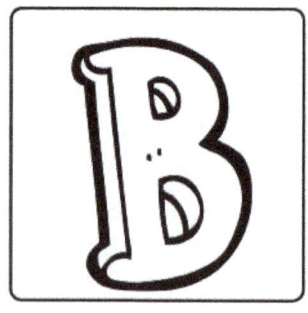 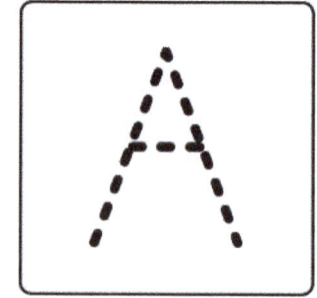 

 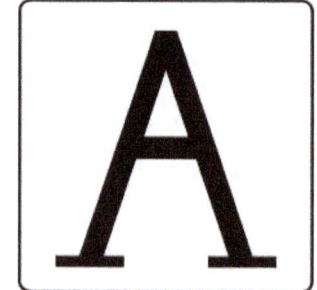 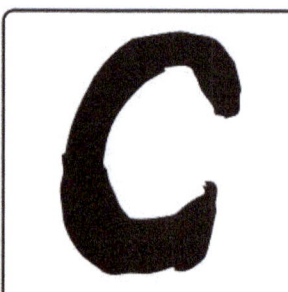

LETTER A

- Say the name of each picture. If it begins with the sound **A**, write **A a** on the line.

A a

and

- Say the word. Then trace the word.

  and and and

- Write the word.

- Fill in the missing letters to write the word.

  a_d   an_   _nd

  __d   a__   _n_

- Complete the sentence with the missing word.

  I love my mom ___ dad.

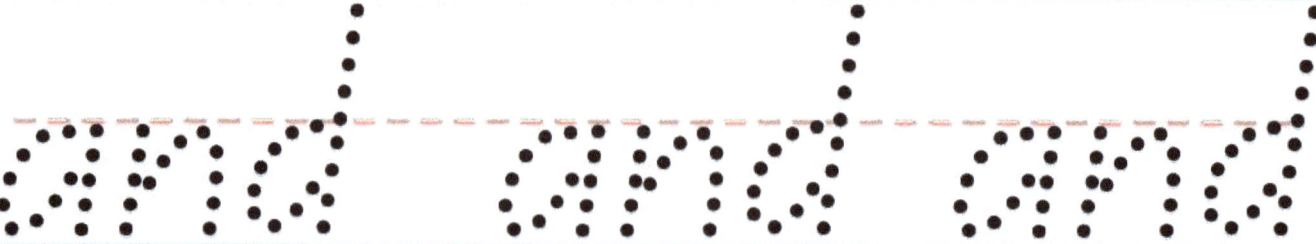

a

- Say the word. Then trace the word.

- Write the word.

- Circle each acorn that has the word **a**.

- Complete the sentence with the missing word.

I see ___ boat.

as

- Say the word. Then trace the word.

as as as as

- Write the word.

- Find and circle the word **as** three times.

a d l k s
s b c x a
s n a s s
c f h i m

- Complete the sentence with the missing word.

Your brother is ___ smart ___ you.

are

- Say the word. Then trace the word.

are are are

- Write the word.

- Color each space that has the word **are**.

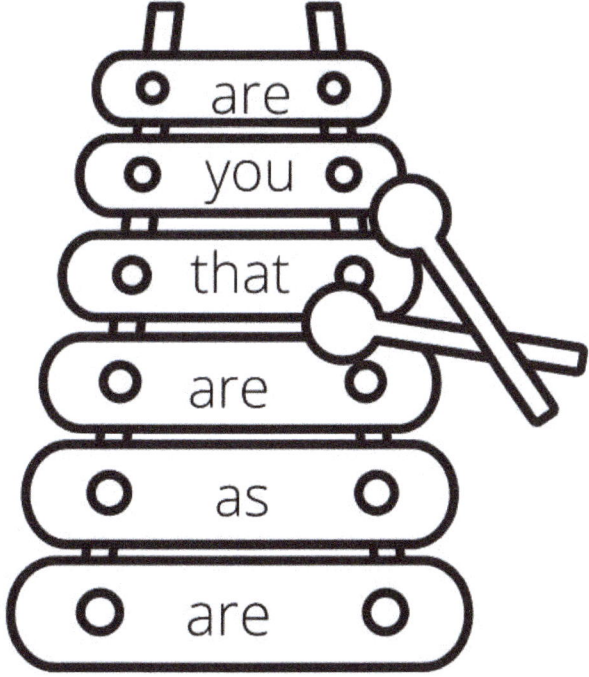

- Complete the sentence with the missing word.

We ___ learning to swim.

LETTER M

Trace the letter **M**:

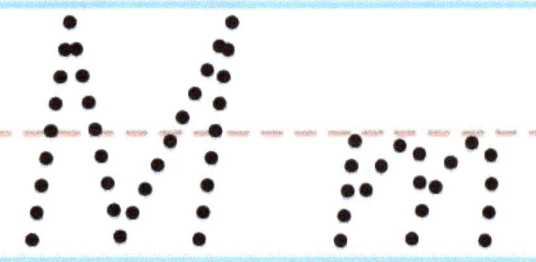

Write an upper and lower case letter **M**:

- Color all the items that begin with the **M** sound:

LETTER M

- Say the name of each picture. Draw a line from the letter **M** to each picture that begins with the **m** sound.

LETTER M

- Trace the letter **M m**. Circle the picture in each row whose name begins with the **m** sound.

LETTER M

- Complete the maze. Color the squares that have the letter **M** printed inside.

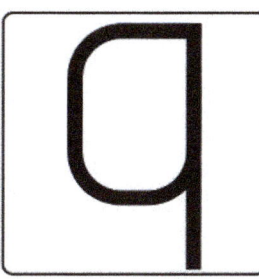

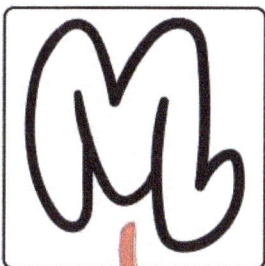

my

- Say the word. Then trace the word.

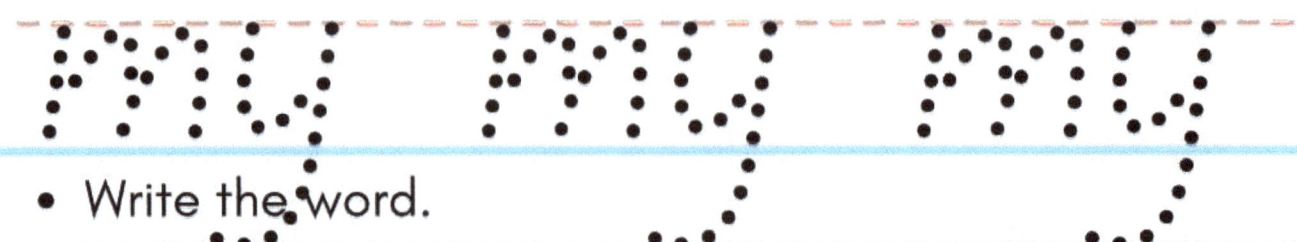

- Write the word.

- Color each space that has the word **my**.

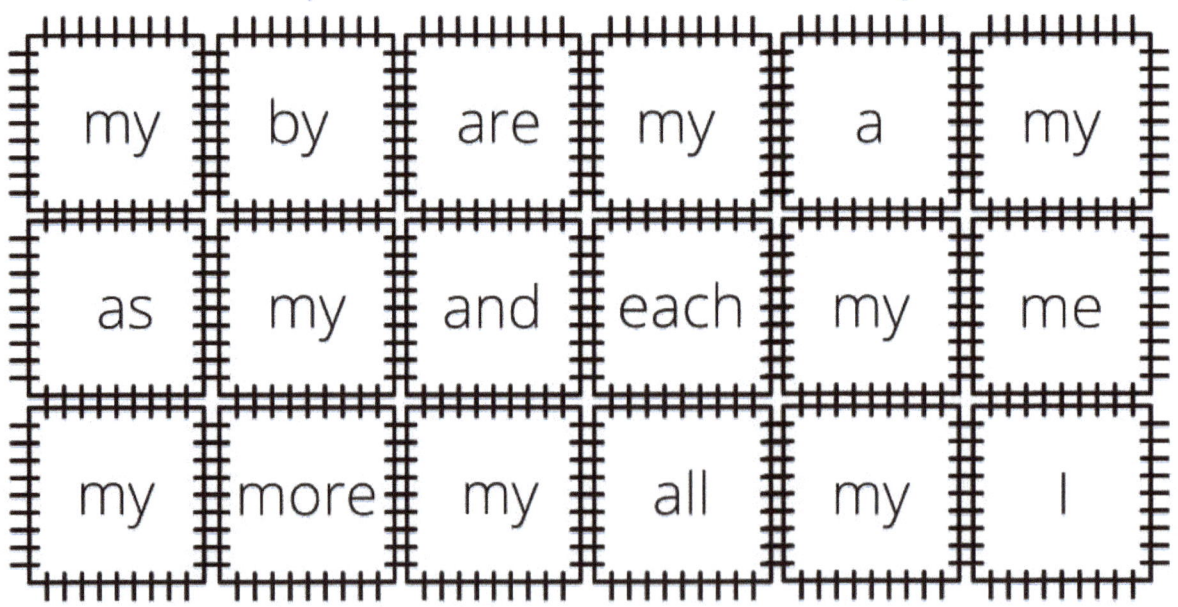

- Complete the sentence with the missing word.

I like ___ dog.

many

- Say the word. Then trace the word.

many   many

- Write the word.

- Fill in the missing letters to write the word.

m__ny   man__

__any

ma__ __   ma__y

- Complete the sentence with the missing word.

I see _____ butterflies.

more

- Say the word. Then trace the word.

more   more

- Write the word.

_____

- Find and circle the word **more** three times.

m d l k s m o r e
o b c x a o d r g
r n a s t r r b a
e f h i m e f m q

- Complete the sentence with the missing word.

I want ____ milk.

15

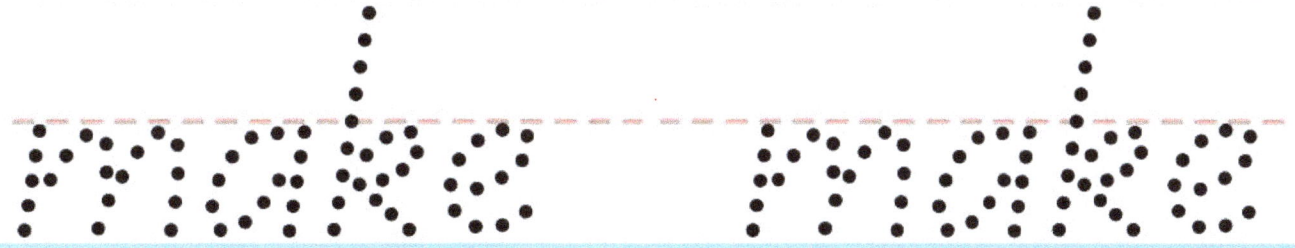

- Say the word. Then trace the word.

  make   make

- Write the word.

- Circle each apple pie that has the word **make**.

- Complete the sentence with the missing word.

You ___ me smile.

LETTER T

Trace the letter **T**:

Write an upper and lower case letter **T**:

- Color all the items that begin with the letter **T**:

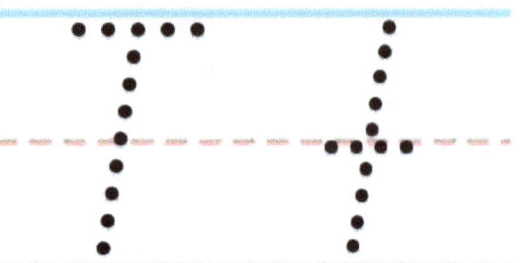

LETTER T

- Trace the letter **T t**. Circle the picture in each row whose name begins with the **t** sound.

LETTER T

- Complete the maze. Color the squares that have the letter **T** printed inside.

  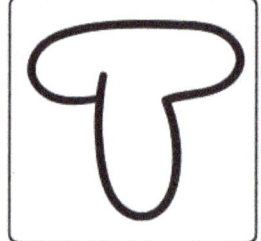

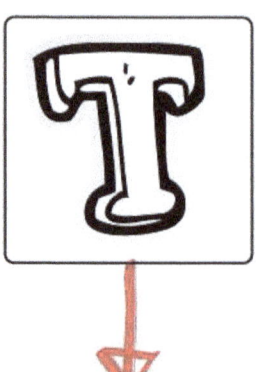 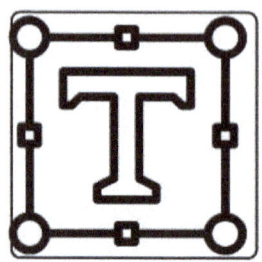 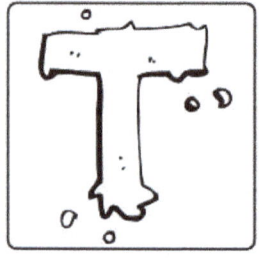

LETTER T

- Say the name of each picture. Draw a line from the letter **T** to each picture that begins with the **t** sound.

to

- Say the word. Then trace the word. Write the word.

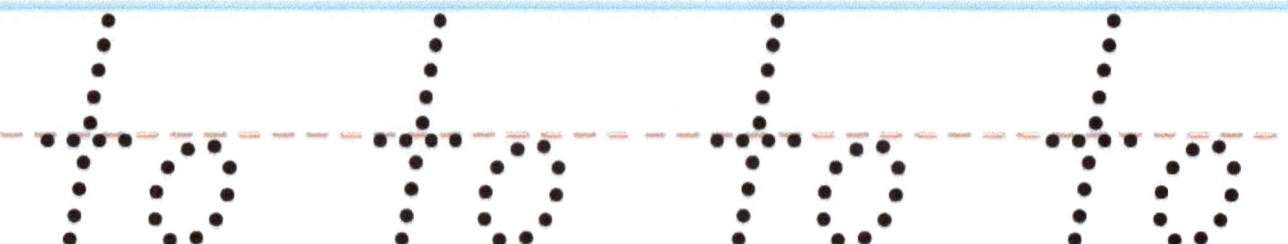

- Color each star that has the word **to**.

- Complete the sentence with the missing word.

I love ___ read.

two

- Say the word. Then trace the word. Write the word.

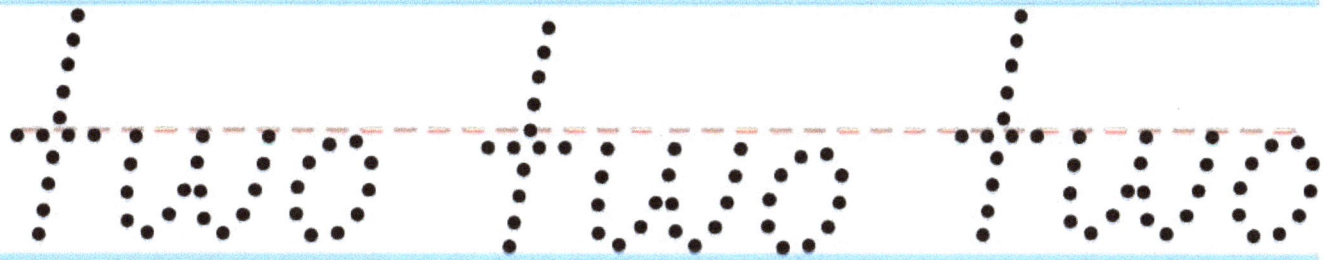

- Find the word **two**. Draw a line to connect the letters.

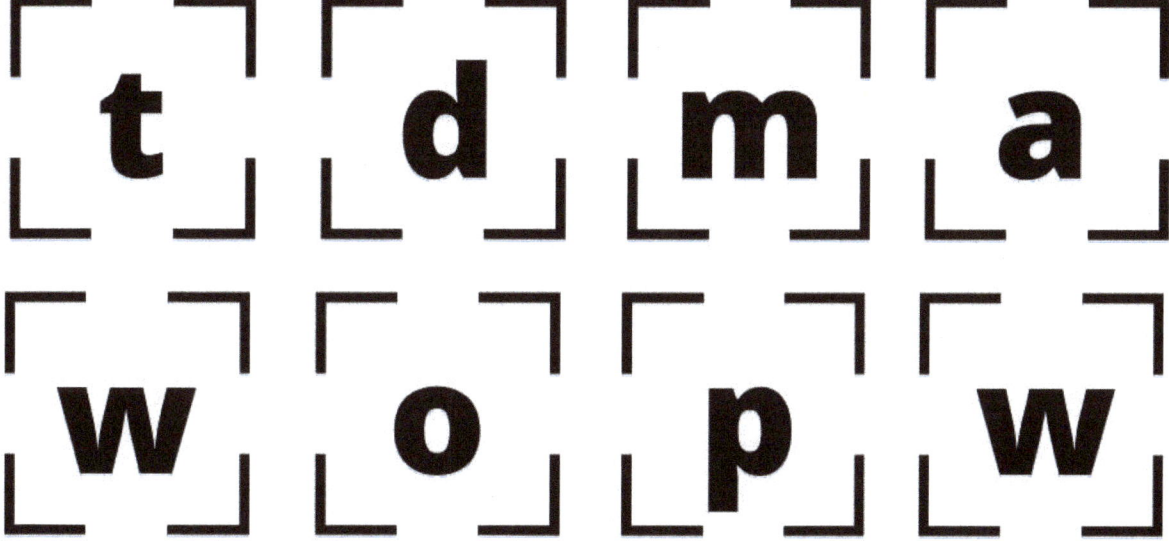

- Complete the sentence with the missing word.

I have ___ hands.

the

- Say the word. Then trace the word. Write the word.

- Fill in the missing letters to write the word.

t_e   _he   th_

_ _e   _h_   t_ _

- Complete the sentence with the missing word.

_____ apple is red.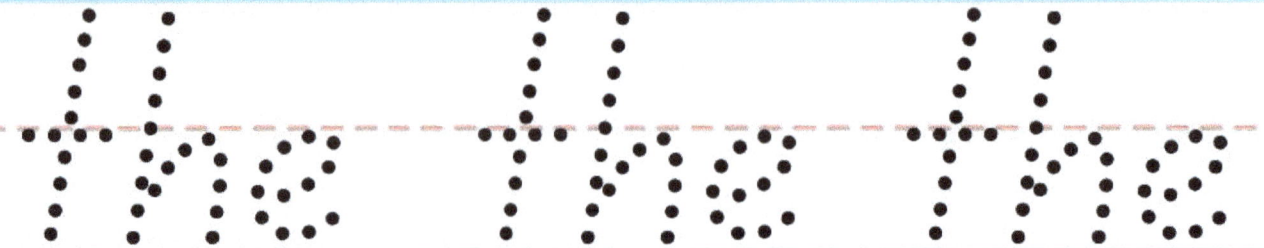

23

this

- Say the word. Then trace the word. Write the word.

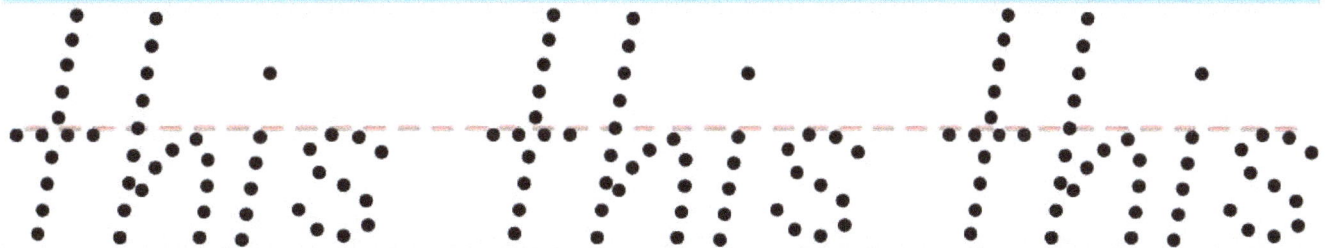

- Find and circle the word **this** three times.

t d l k s m o r t
h **t h i s** o d r h
i n a s t r r b i
s f **h i m** e f m s

- Complete the sentence with the missing word.

_____ is my cat.

LETTER S

Trace the letter S:

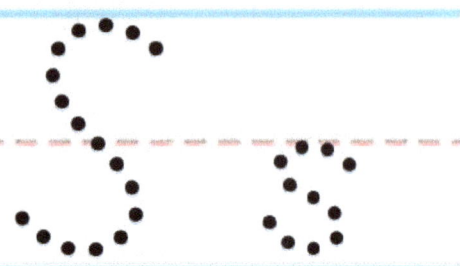

Write an upper and lower case letter S:

- Color all the items that begin with the letter S:

LETTER S

- Trace the letter **S s**. Circle the picture in each row whose name begins with the **s** sound.

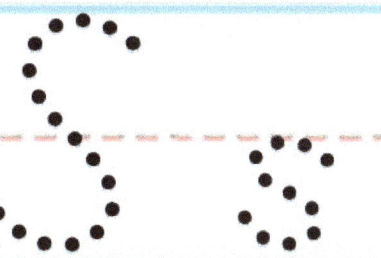   

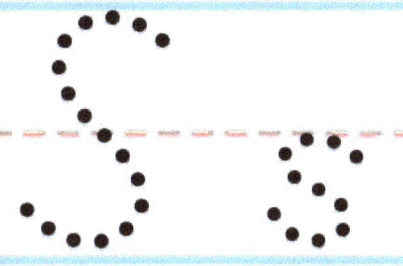   

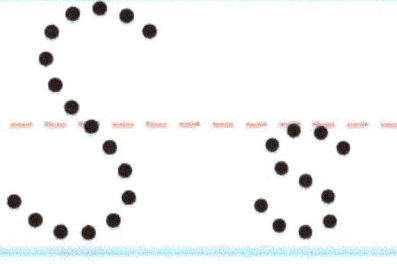   

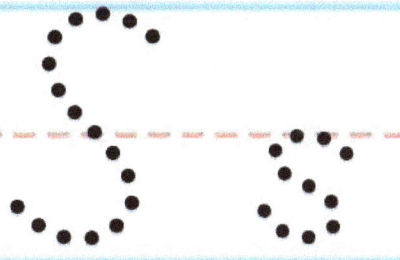   

LETTER S

- Say the name of each picture. Draw an **X** on each picture that begins with the **S** sound:

LETTER S

- Trace the letter **S s**. Say the name of each picture. Draw a line from letter **Ss** to each picture that begins with the **s** sound.

see

- Say the word. Then trace the word. Write the word.

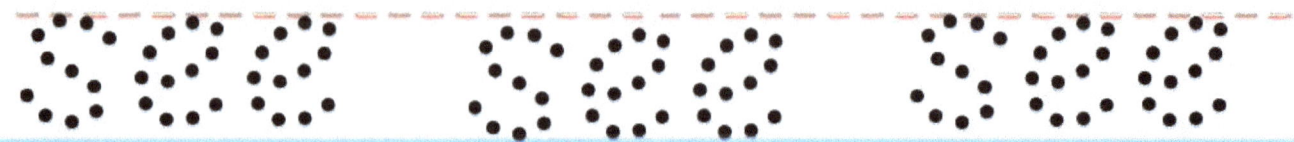

- Color each space that has the word **see**.

- Complete the sentence with the missing word.

I _____ a blue boat.

she

- Say the word. Then trace the word. Write the word.

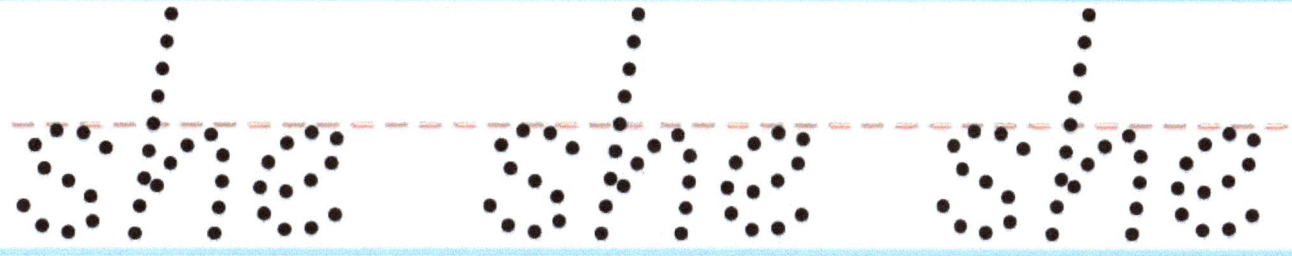

- Find the word **she**. Draw a line to connect the letters.

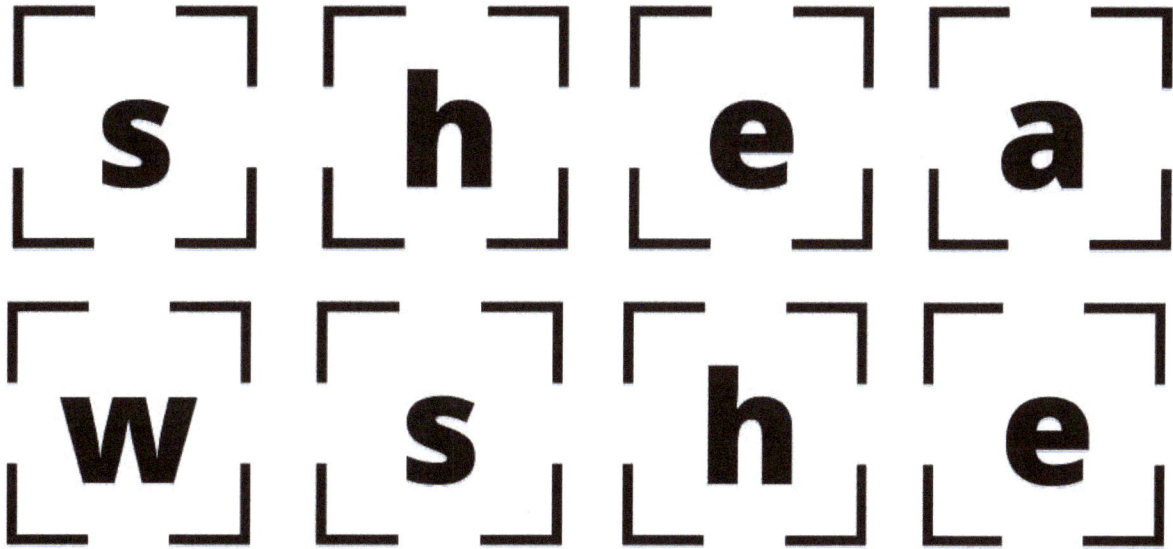

- Complete the sentence with the missing word.

_____ is my sister.

so

- Say the word. Then trace the word. Write the word.

- Circle each fish that has the word **so**.

- Complete the sentence with the missing word.

Ice cream is ___ yummy!

some

- Say the word. Then trace the word. Write the word.

some   some

- Fill in the missing letters to write the word **some**.

som_   _ome

so__e   s___e

_o__e   s____

- Complete the sentence with the missing word.

I want ____ milk.

LETTER I

Trace the letter **I**:

Write an upper and lower case letter **I**:

- Color all the items that begin with the letter **I**:

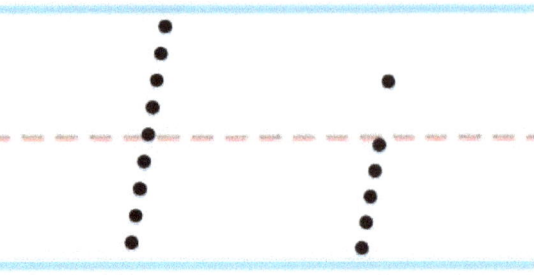

LETTER I

- Trace the letter **I i**. Circle the picture in each row whose name begins with the **i** sound.

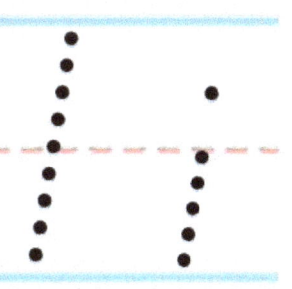   

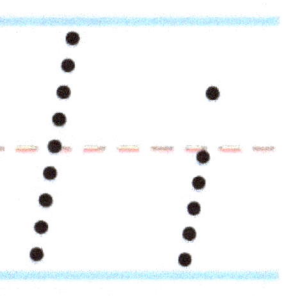   

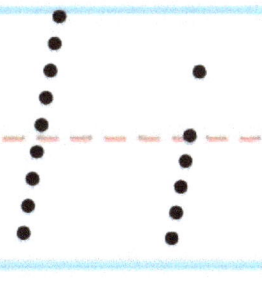   

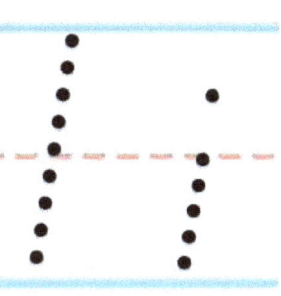   

LETTER I

- Say the name of each picture. Draw a line from letter S to each picture that begins with the s sound.

LETTER I

- Complete the maze. Color the squares that have the letter I printed inside.

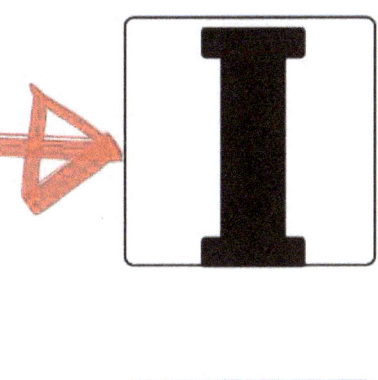
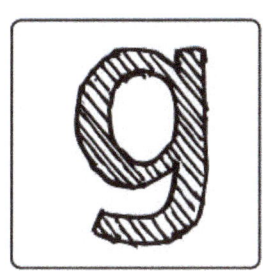

I

- Say the word. Then trace the word. Write the word.

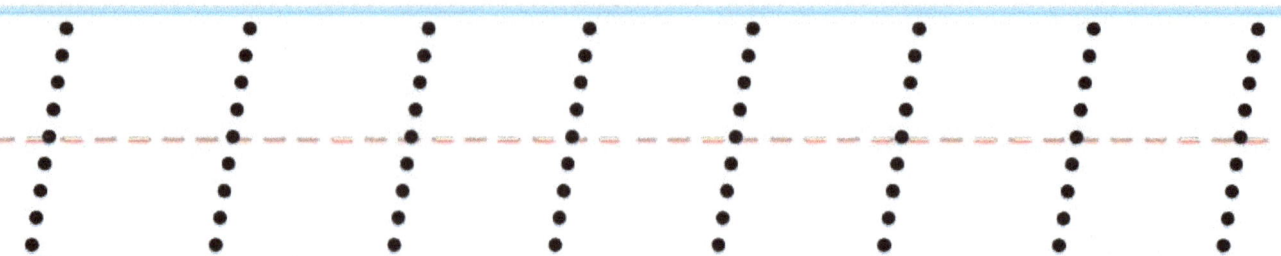

- Color each space that has the word **I**.

i	I	are	i	a	my
I	two	and	I	this	make
my	she	into	all	my	I

- Complete the sentence with the missing word.

___ like to write.

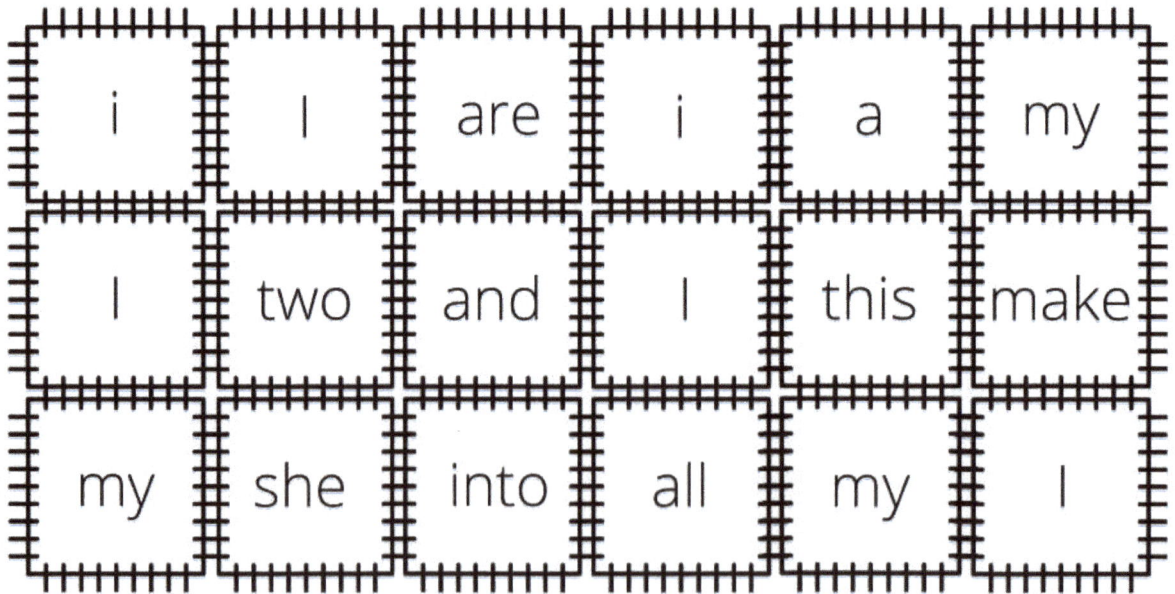

is

- Say the word. Then trace the word. Write the word.

- Color each cloud that has the word **is**.

- Complete the sentence with the missing word.

This ___ my home.

into

- Say the word. Then trace the word. Write the word.

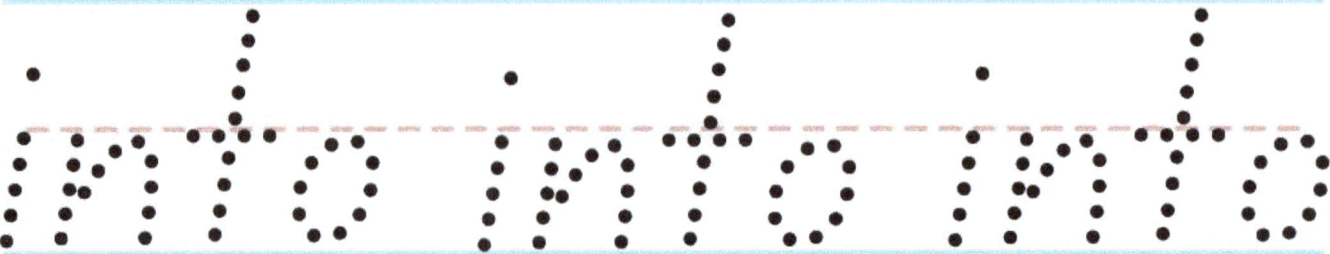

- Find the word **into**. Draw a line to connect the letters.

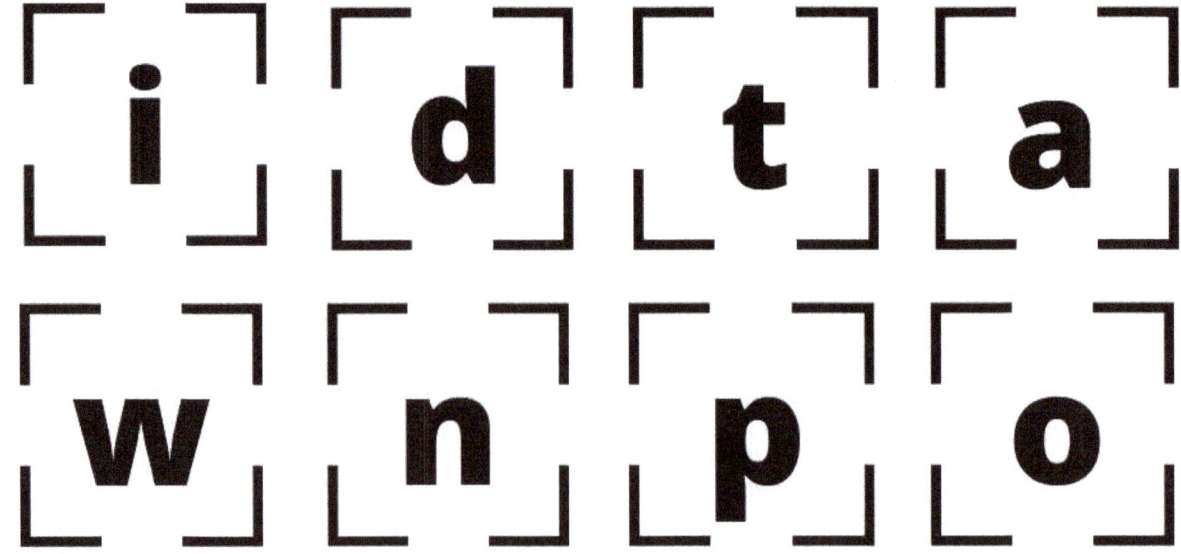

- Complete the sentence with the missing word.

Put the toys _____ the box.

it

- Say the word. Then trace the word. Write the word.

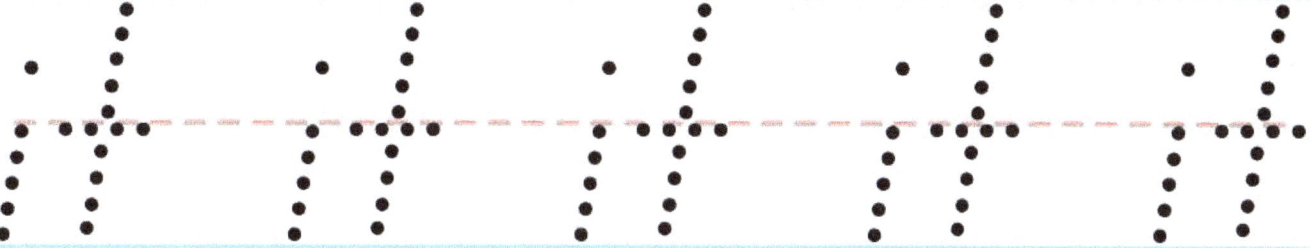

- Circle each hamburger that has the word **it**.

- Complete the sentence with the missing word.

___ is cloudy.

LETTER F

Trace the letter **F f**:

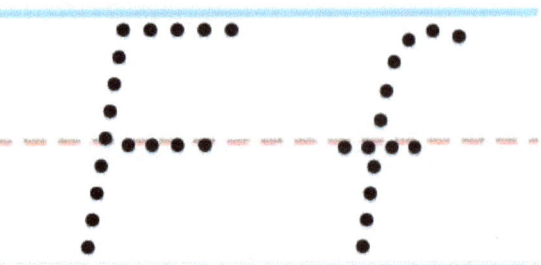

Write an upper and lower case letter F:

- Color all the items that begin with the letter **F**:

41

LETTER F

- Trace the letter **F f**. Circle the picture in each row whose name begins with the **f** sound.

LETTER F

- Say the name of each picture. Circle each picture that begins with the sound **F**:

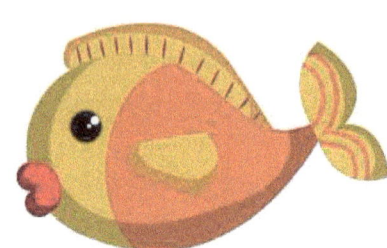

LETTER F

- Complete the maze. Color the squares that have the letter **F** printed inside.

find

- Say the word. Then trace the word. Write the word.

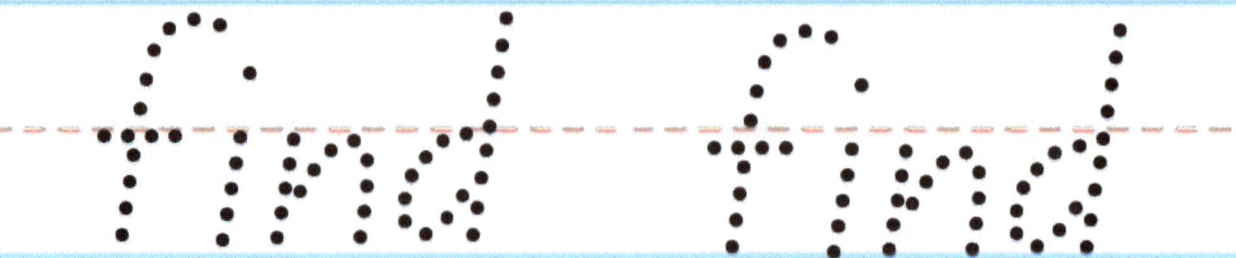

- Color each space that has the word **find**.

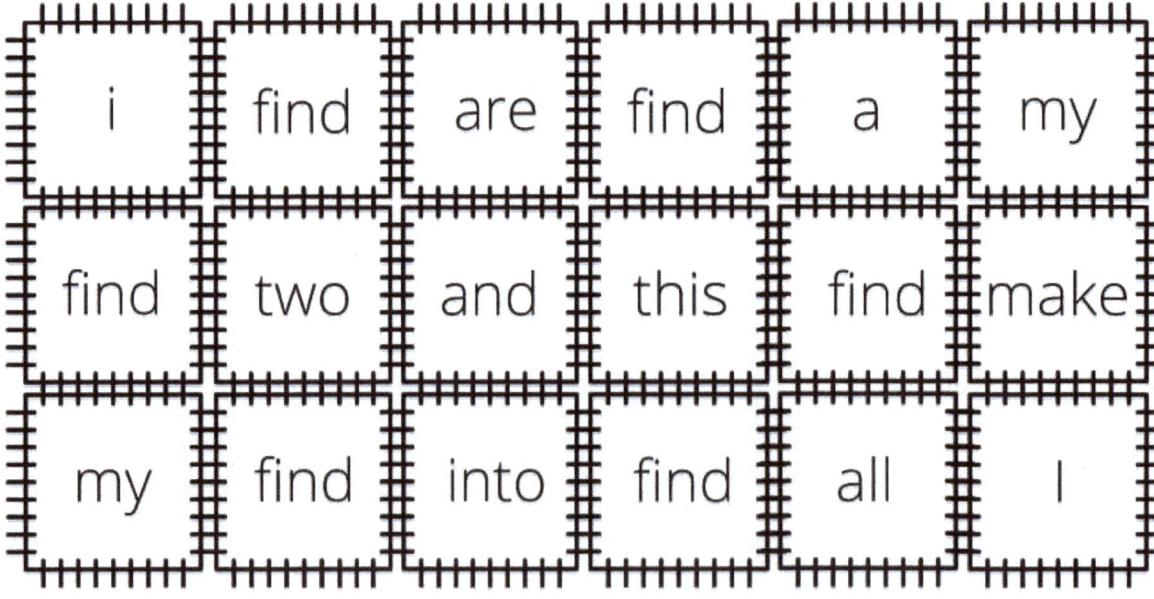

i	find	are	find	a	my
find	two	and	this	find	make
my	find	into	find	all	I

- Complete the sentence with the missing word.

I _____ a dog.

for

- Say the word. Then trace the word. Write the word.

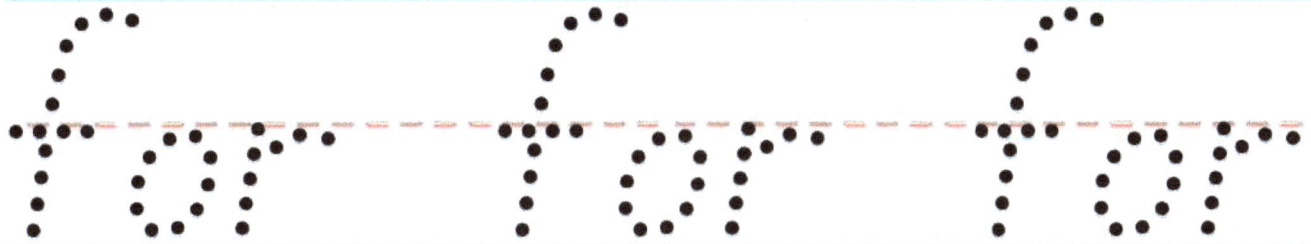

- Color each tree that has the word **for**.

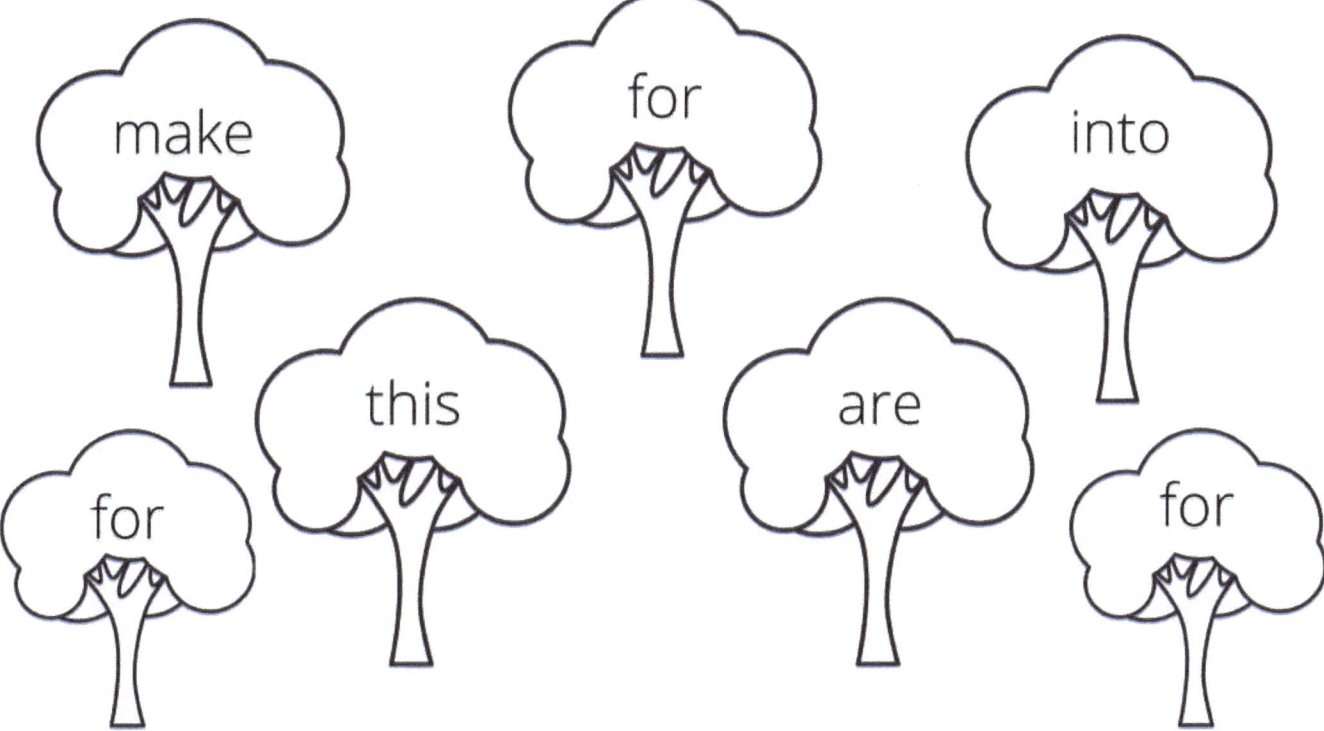

- Complete the sentence with the missing word.

This is ___ you.

from

- Say the word. Then trace the word. Write the word.

from   from

- Fill in the missing letter to write the word **from**.

f_om   fr_m   fro_

_ _ om   f_ _ m

_rom   _ _ _m

- Complete the sentence with the missing word.

Where are you ____

47

first

- Say the word. Then trace the word. Write the word.

- Find and circle the word **first** tree times.

f i r s t m o r f
i t h i s o d r i
r n a s t r r b r
s f h i m e f m s
t y h i s o d r t

- Complete the sentence with the missing word.

My _____ name is...

LETTER D

Trace the letter **D d**:

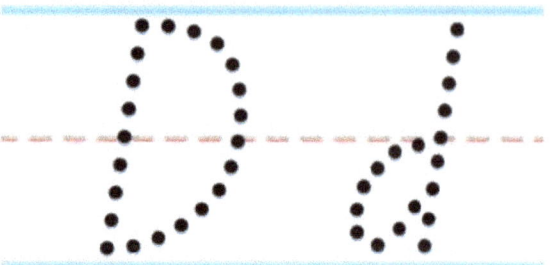

Write an upper and lower case letter **D**:

- Color all the items that begin with the letter **D**:

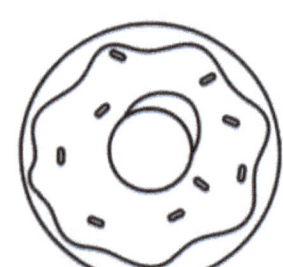

LETTER D

- Trace the letter **D d**. Circle the picture in each row whose name begins with the **d** sound.

LETTER D

- Complete the maze. Color the squares that have the letter **D** printed inside.

51

LETTER D

- Say the name of each picture. Draw an **X** on each picture that begins with the **D** sound:

do

- Say the word. Then trace the word. Write the word.

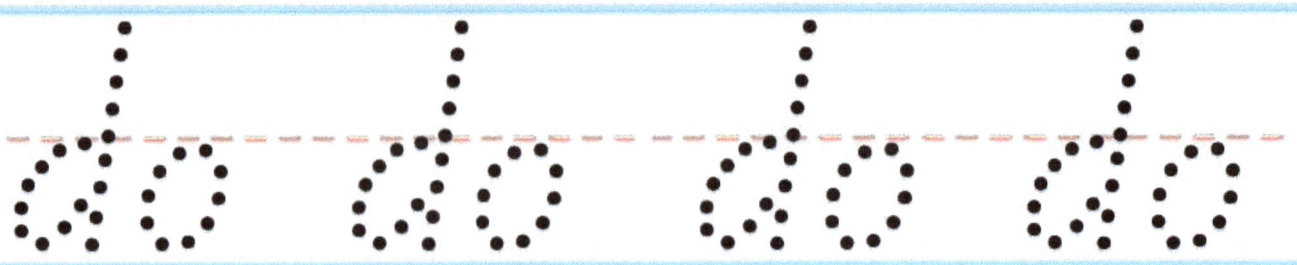

- Color each space that has the word **do**.

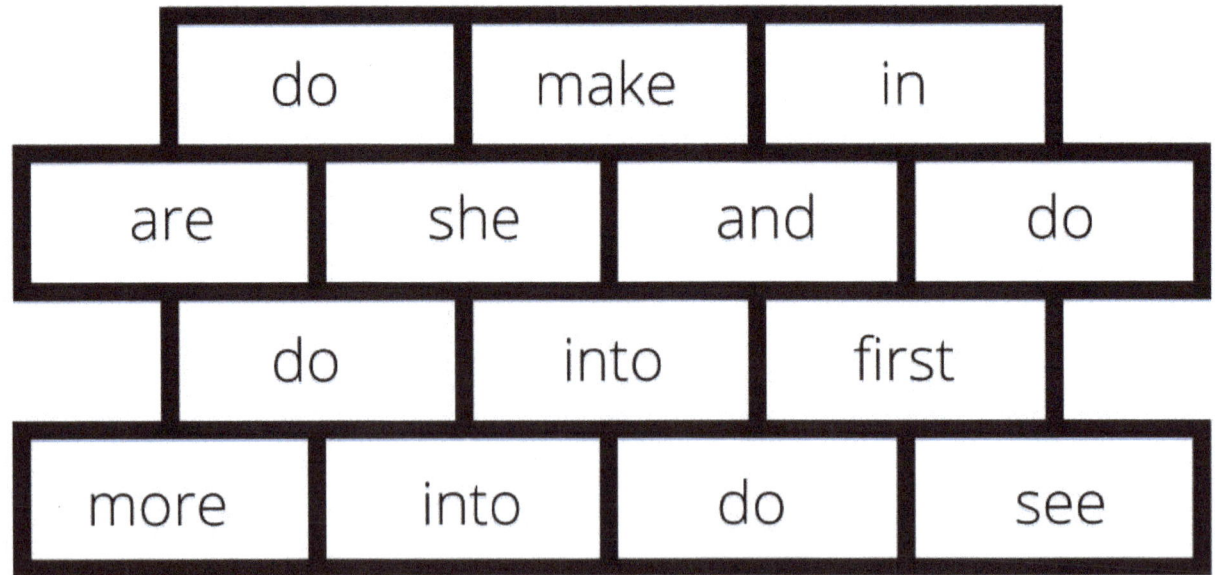

- Complete the sentence with the missing word.

___ you like dogs or cats?

did

- Say the word. Then trace the word. Write the word.

did   did   did

- Find the word **did**. Draw a line to connect the letters.

| s | i | t | a |
| d | m | d | w |

- Complete the sentence with the missing word.

____ you liked the movie?

54

day

- Say the word. Then trace the word. Write the word.

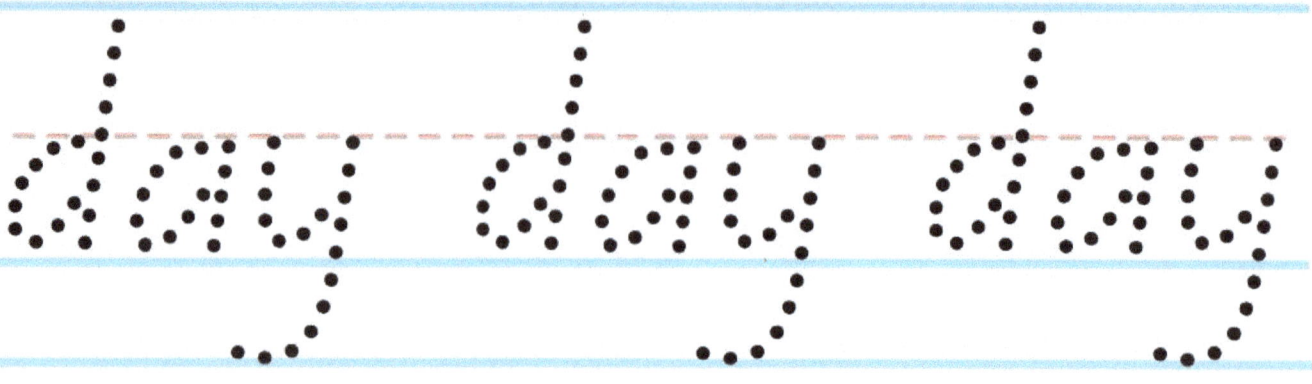

- Circle each image that has the word **day**.

- Complete the sentence with the missing word.

What _____ is today?

down

- Say the word. Then trace the word. Write the word.

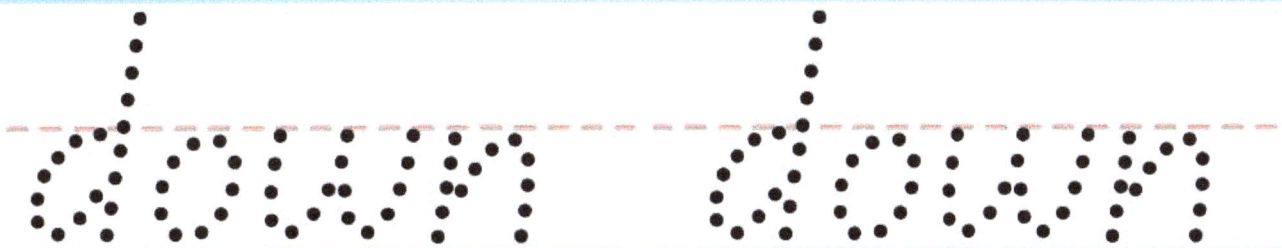

- Fill in the missing letters to write the word **down**.

dow_   **_own**

do__n   **d__n**

_o__n   **d___**

- Complete the sentence with the missing word.

Get ____ the table!

LETTER R

Trace the letter **R**:

Write an upper and lower case letter **R**:

- Color all the items that begin with the **R** sound:

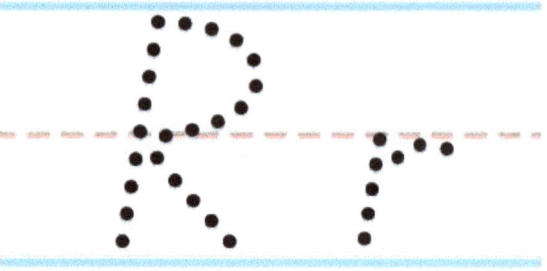

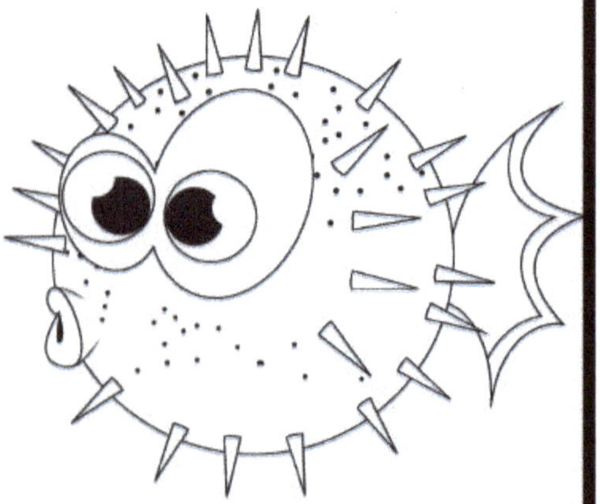

LETTER R

- Say the name of each picture. Circle each picture that begins with the **r** sound.

LETTER R

- Color only the squares with letter **R**.

 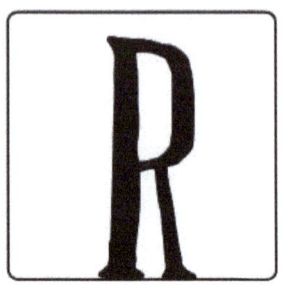 

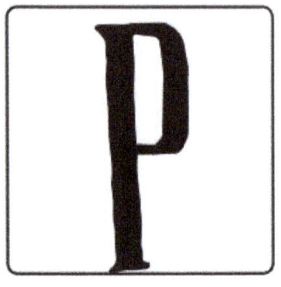  

LETTER R

- Say the name of each picture. If it begins with the sound **R**, write **R r** on the line.

run

- Say the word. Then trace the word.

run run run

- Circle each baloon that has the word **run**.

- Complete the sentence with the missing word.

We like to ____.

ride

- Say the word. Then trace the word.

  ride   ride

- Write the word.

- Fill in the missing letters to write the word.

r_de   _ide   rid_

__de   r_d_   ri___

___e   _i__   __r__

- Complete the sentence with the missing word.

I ____ my bike.

LETTER O

Trace the letter O o:

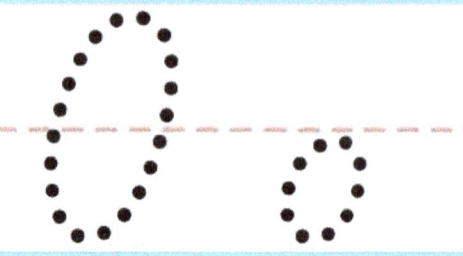

Write an upper and lower case letter O:

- Color all the items that begin with the O sound:

LETTER O

- Say the name of each picture. Draw a line from the letter O to each picture that begins with the o sound.

LETTER O

- Trace the letter O o. Circle the picture in each row whose name begins with the o sound.

LETTER O

- Say the name of each picture. Draw an **X** on each picture that begins with the **O** sound:

on

- Say the word. Then trace the word. Write the word.

- Color each space that has the word **on**.

- Complete the sentence with the missing word.

The mug is ___ the table.

of

- Say the word. Then trace the word. Write the word.

  of of of of of

- Find the word **of**. Draw a line to connect the letters.

  o f e m

  s o f e

- Complete the sentence with the missing word.

I see a cup ___ tea.

out

- Say the word. Then trace the word. Write the word.

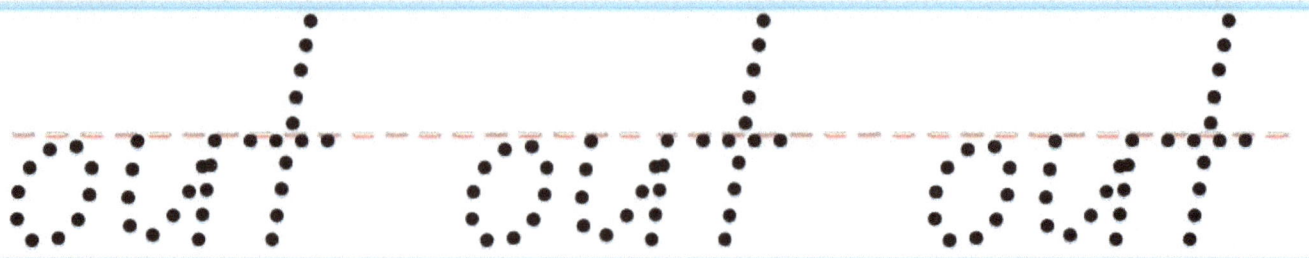

- How many times can you find the word **out**.

☐ times

- Complete the sentence with the missing word.

Come ____ and play!

over

- Say the word. Then trace the word. Write the word.

over   over

- Fill in the missing letters to write the word **over**.

ove_   _ver

ov_r   o_ _r

_v_r   o_ _ _

- Complete the sentence with the missing word.

The book is ___ there.

LETTER G

Trace the letter **G g**:

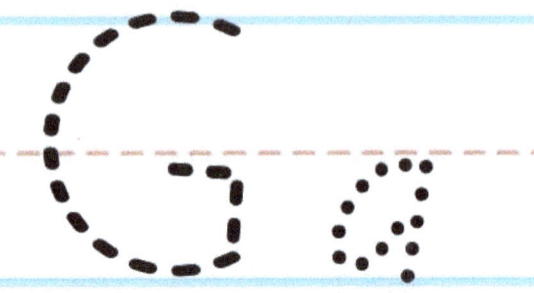

Write an upper and lower case letter **G**:

- Color all the items that begin with the letter **G**:

LETTER G

- Say the name of each picture. Circle each picture that begins with the **g** sound.

LETTER G

- Complete the maze. Color the squares that have the letter **G** printed inside.

LETTER G

- Say the name of each picture. Draw a line from the letter **G** to each picture that begins with the **g** sound.

go

- Say the word. Then trace the word. Write the word.

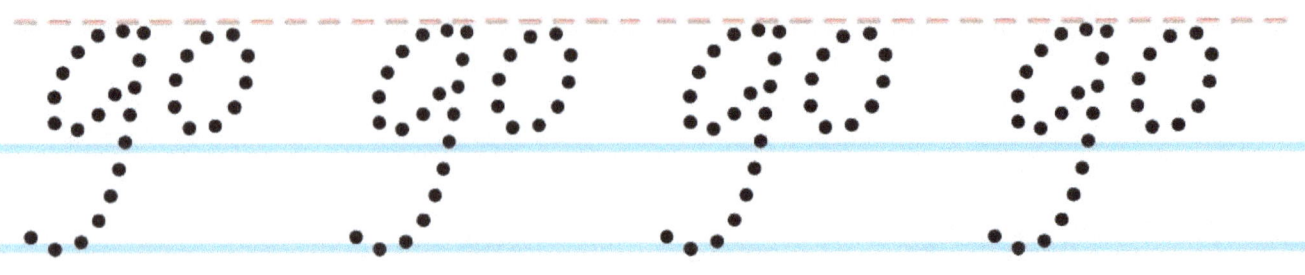

- Color each star that has the word **go**.

- Complete the sentence with the missing word.

I can ___ for a walk.

get

- Say the word. Then trace the word. Write the word.

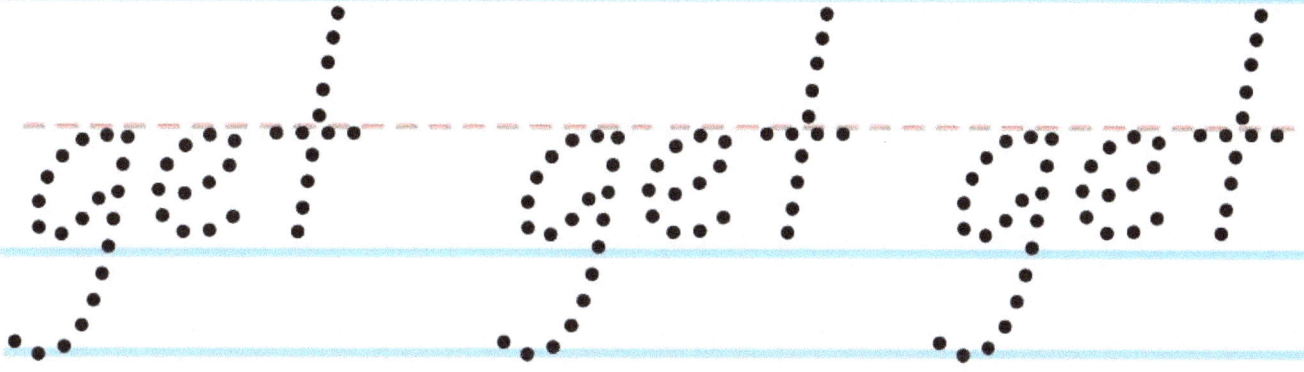

- Find the word **get**. Draw a line to connect the letters.

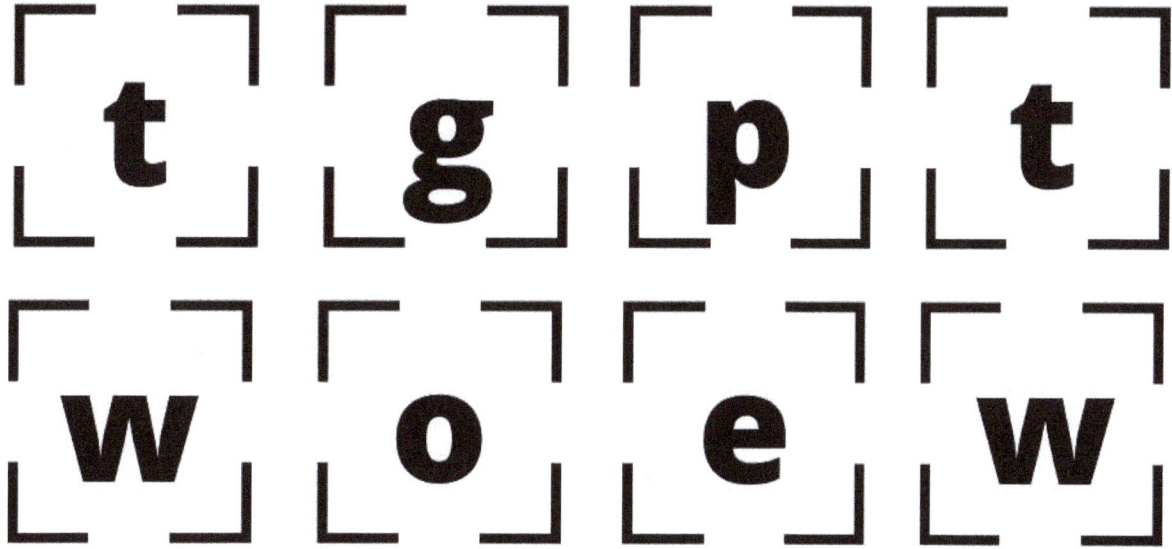

- Complete the sentence with the missing word.

I'll _____ the bill.

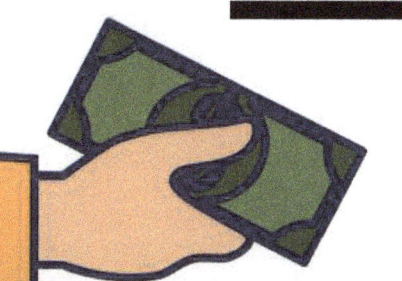

good

- Say the word. Then trace the word. Write the word.

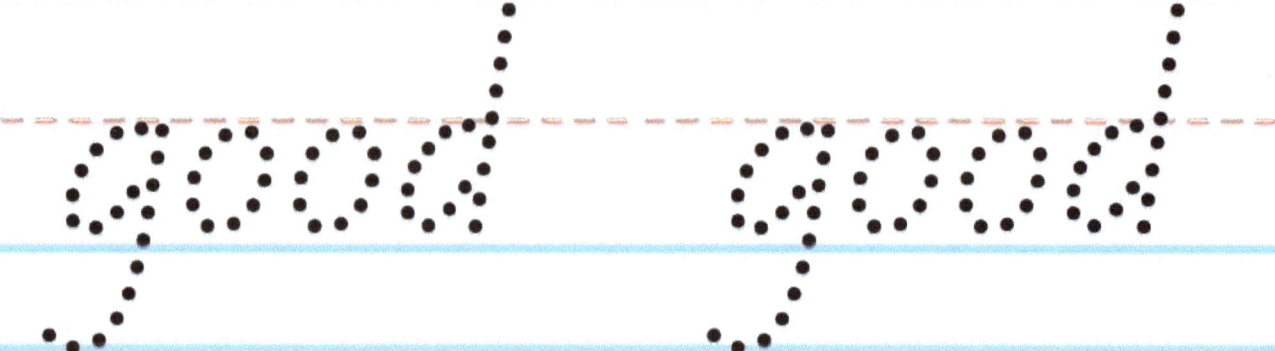

- Fill in the missing letters to write the word.

g_od

goo_

_ood

g_ _d

go_ _

_ _ _d

- Complete the sentence with the missing word.

Ice cream is so ___.

green

- Say the word. Then trace the word. Write the word.

green green

- Find and circle the word **this** three times.

G d l k g r e e n
g r e e n o d r h
o n a s t r r b i
s f g r e e n m s

- Complete the sentence with the missing word.

My hat is _____.

LETTER L

Trace the letter L l:

Write an upper and lower case letter L:

• Color all the items that begin with the letter L:

LETTER L

- Trace the letter **L l**. Circle the picture in each row whose name begins with the **l** sound.

LETTER L

- Say the name of each picture. Draw an **X** on each picture that begins with the **L** sound:

LETTER L

- Trace the letter **L l**. Say the name of each picture. Draw a line from letter **Ll** to each picture that begins with the **L** sound.

like

- Say the word. Then trace the word. Write the word.

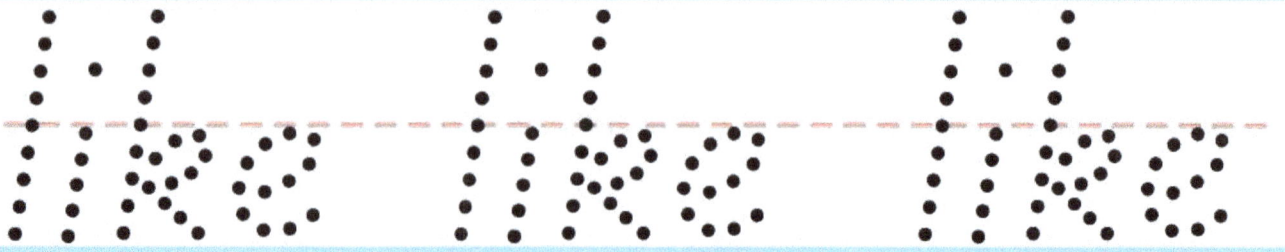

- Color each space that has the word **like**.

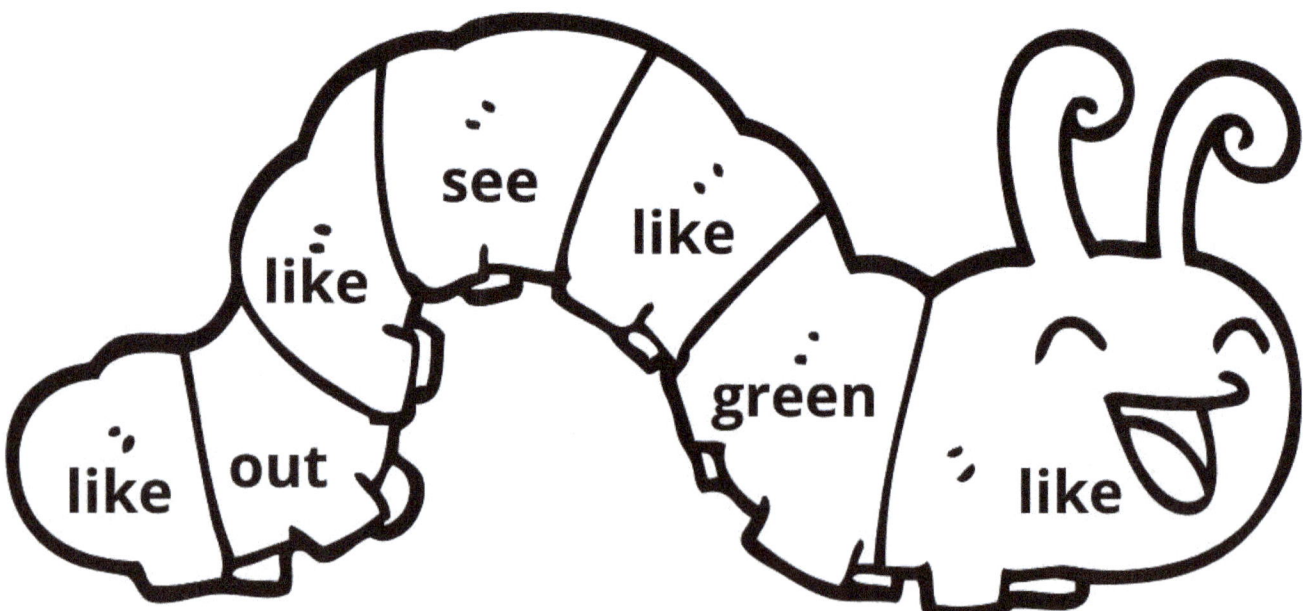

- Complete the sentence with the missing word.

I _____ my kitty.

look

- Say the word. Then trace the word. Write the word.

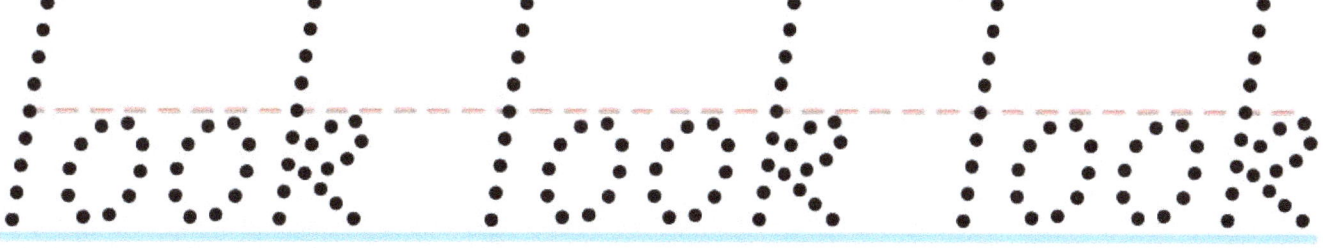

- Find the word **look**. Draw a line to connect the letters.

- Complete the sentence with the missing word.

____ at my sister!

long

- Say the word. Then trace the word. Write the word.

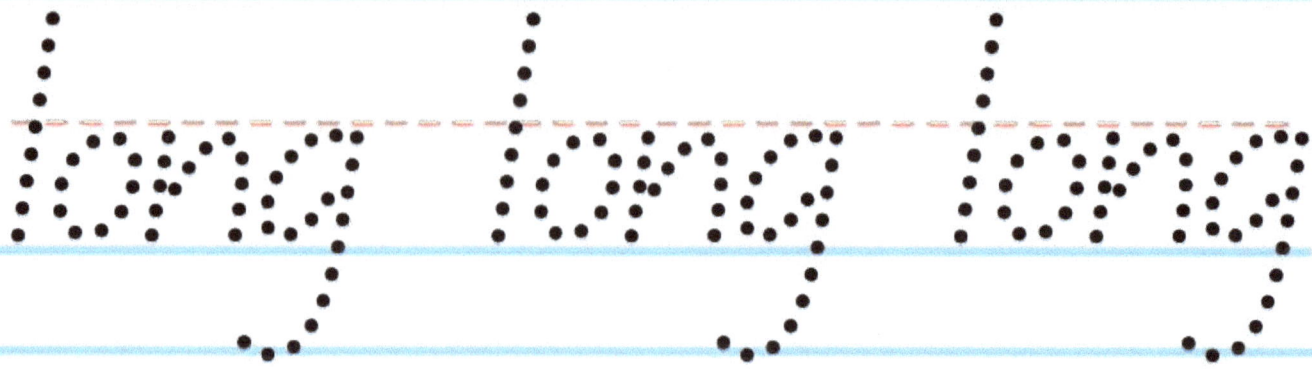

- Circle each mug that has the word **long**.

- Complete the sentence with the missing word.

I have ____ hair.

little

- Say the word. Then trace the word. Write the word.

  little   little

- Fill in the missing letters to write the word **little**.

  li_ _le   _ittl_

  _ _tt_ _   l_ _ _le

  _ _ _ _ _e   li_ _ _ _

- Complete the sentence with the missing word.

  I see a _____ girl.

LETTER H

Trace the letter **H h**:

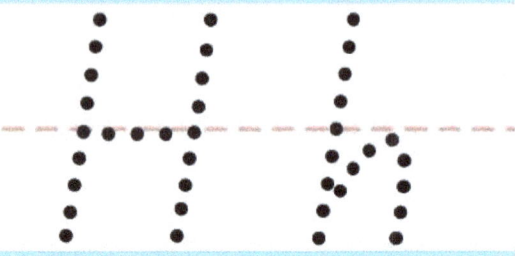

Write an upper and lower case letter **H**:

- Color all the items that begin with the letter **H**:

LETTER H

- Trace the letter **H h**. Circle the picture in each row whose name begins with the **h** sound.

LETTER H

- Say the name of each picture. Draw a line from letter **H** to each picture that begins with the **h** sound.

LETTER H

- Complete the maze. Color the squares that have the letter **H** printed inside.

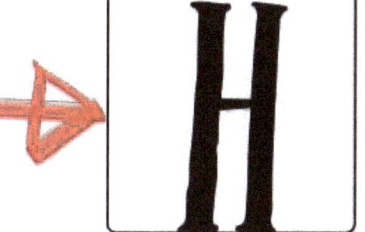  

 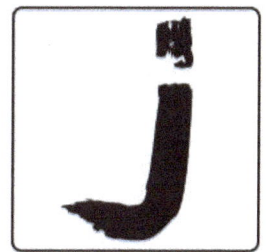 

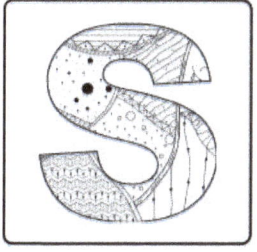  

 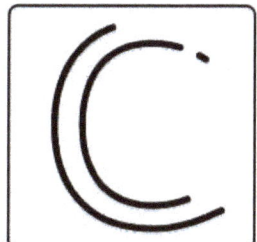 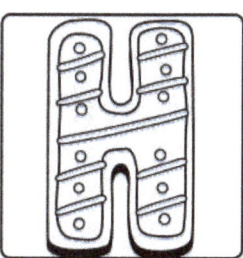

he

- Say the word. Then trace the word. Write the word.

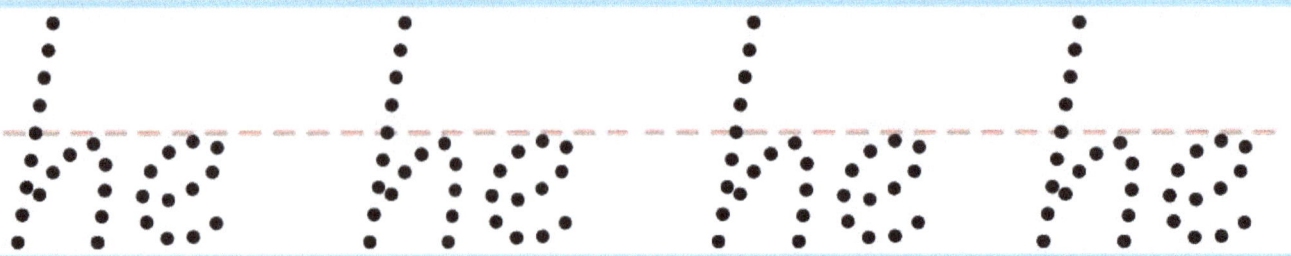

- Color each space that has the word **he**.

- Complete the sentence with the missing word.

___ **likes to run.**

here

- Say the word. Then trace the word. Write the word.

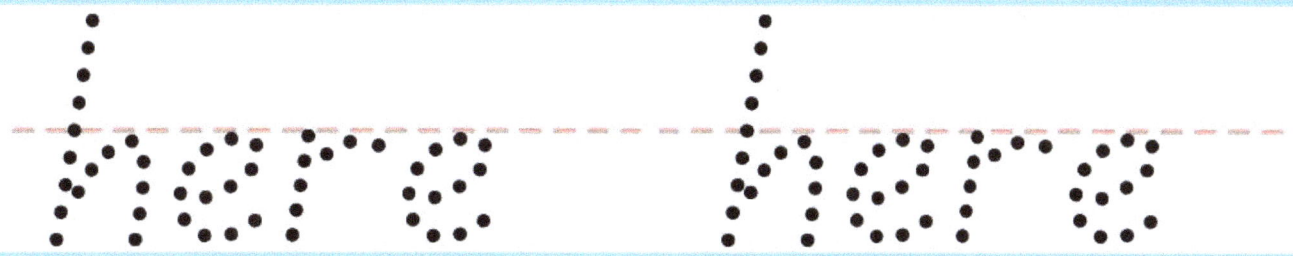

- Color each cloud that has the word **here**.

- Complete the sentence with the missing word.

My bus is _____

have

- Say the word. Then trace the word. Write the word.

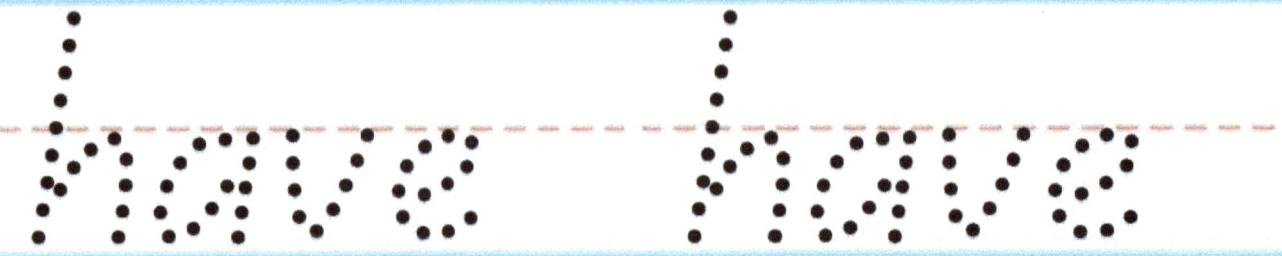

- Find the word **have**. Draw a line to connect the letters.

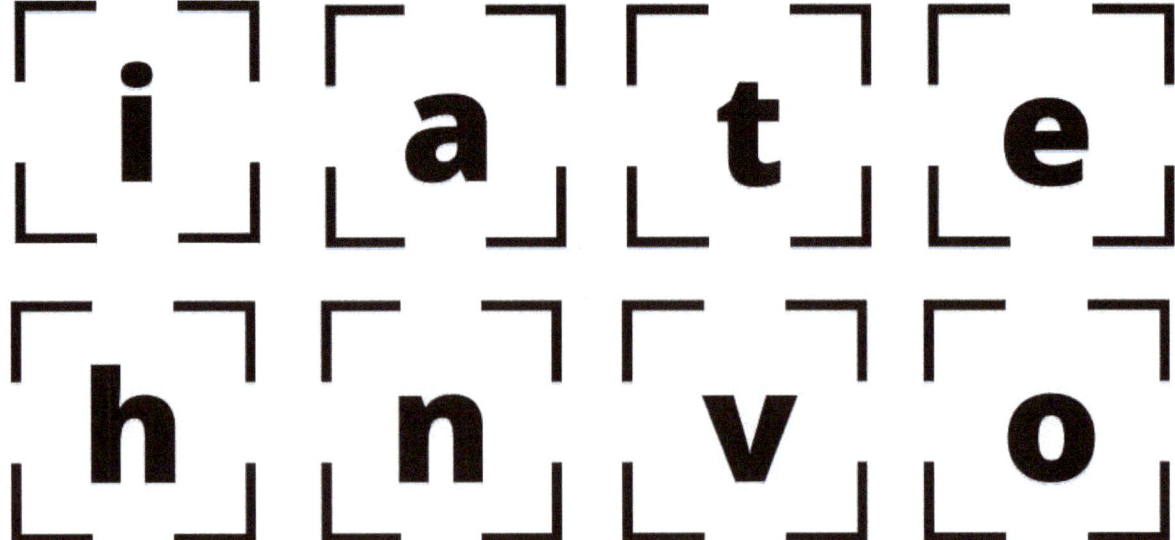

- Complete the sentence with the missing word.

I _____ a fish.

how

- Say the word. Then trace the word. Write the word.

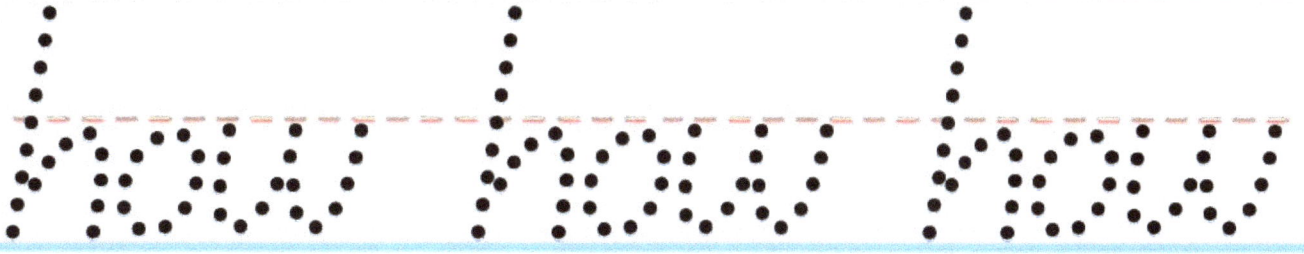

- Circle each fish that has the word **how**.

- Complete the sentence with the missing word.

_____ do you do?

LETTER U

Trace the letter **U u**:

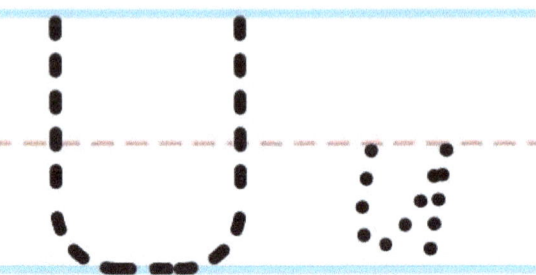

Write an upper and lower case letter **U**:

- Color all the items that begin with the letter **U**:

LETTER U

- Trace the letter **U u**. Circle the picture in each row whose name begins with the **U** sound.

LETTER U

- Say the name of each picture. Trace the letter **u** to complete each word.

up

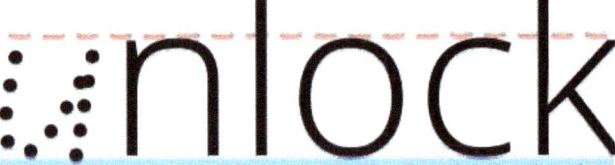
unlock

uncle

under

LETTER U

- Complete the maze. Color the squares that have the letter **U** printed inside.

 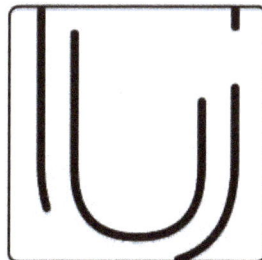 

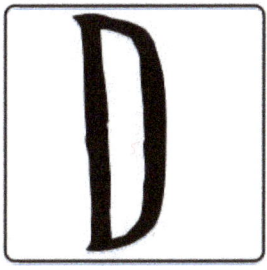 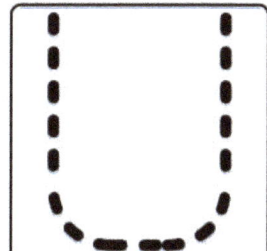 

use

- Say the word. Then trace the word. Write the word.

- Color each space that has the word **use**.

use	find	are	use	over	my
and	two	use	this	use	make
my	use	into	like	all	use

- Complete the sentence with the missing word.

I _____ a fork.

up

- Say the word. Then trace the word. Write the word.

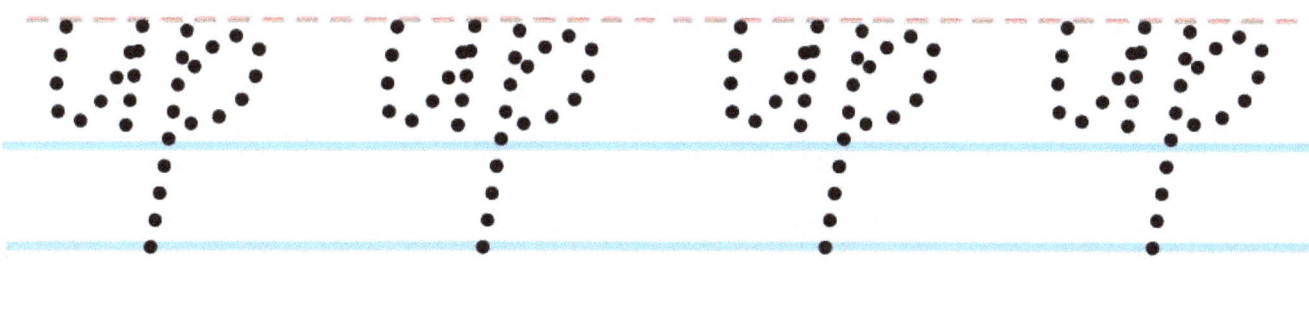

- Color each step that has the word **up**.

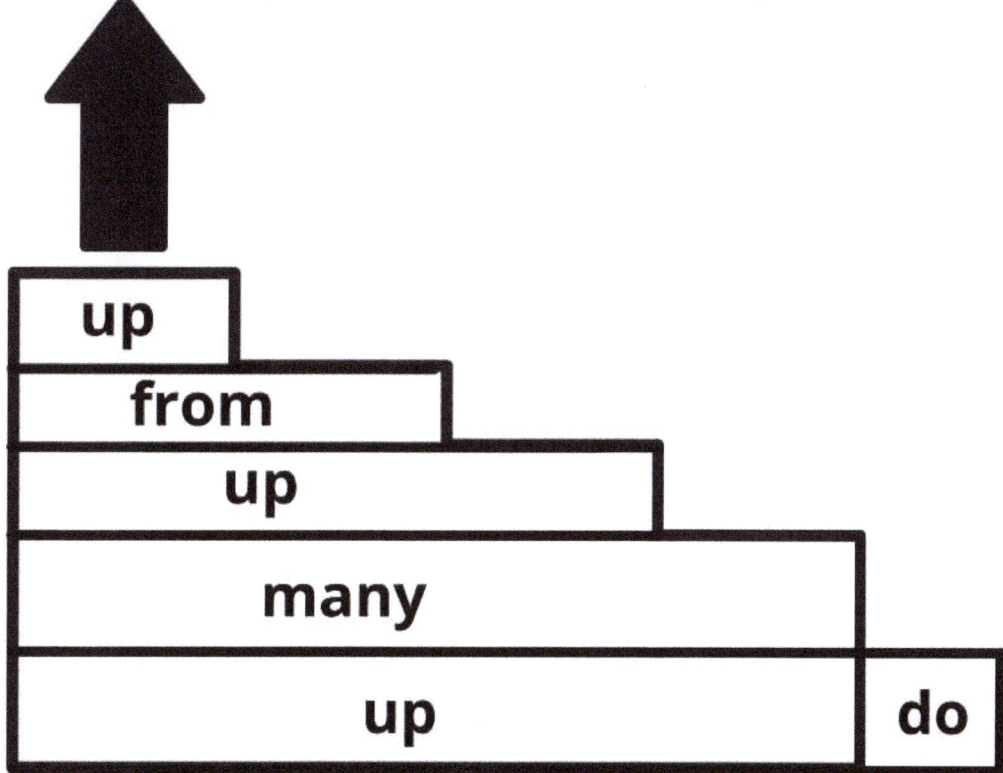

- Complete the sentence with the missing word.

The sun is ___.

LETTER C

Trace the letter **C c**:

Write an upper and lower case letter **C**:

- Color all the items that begin with the **C** sound:

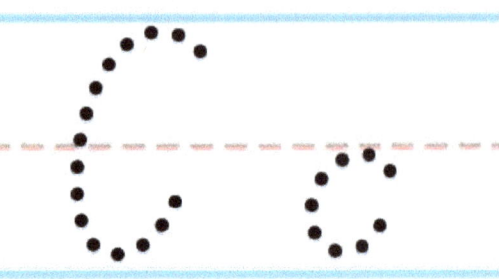

LETTER C

- Say the name of each picture. Circle each picture that begins with the **C** sound.

LETTER C

- Say the name of each picture. Trace the letter **c** to complete each word.

 cat
 clown

crab
 can

LETTER C

- Say the name of each picture. If it begins with the sound **C**, write **C c** on the line.

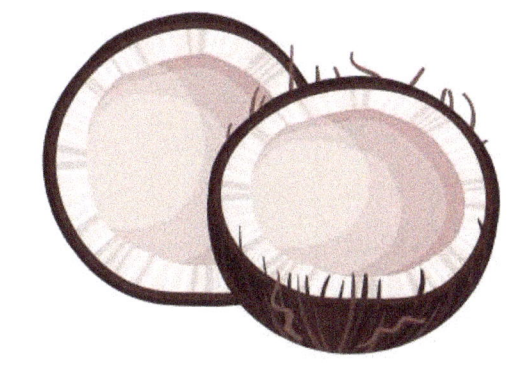

can

- Say the word. Then trace the word.

  can   can   can

- Write the word.

- Fill in the missing letters to write the word.

  c_n   ca_   _an

  __n   c__   _a_

- Complete the sentence with the missing word.

  I ___ swim.

come

- Say the word. Then trace the word.

  come   come

- Write the word.

- Circle each acorn that has the word **come**.

  come   in   of   come

  here   come   look   on

- Complete the sentence with the missing word.

  _____ and play with me.

call

- Say the word. Then trace the word.

  call   call   call

- Write the word.

- Find and circle the word **call** three times.

  c a l l c
  a b c x a
  l n a s l
  l f h i l

- Complete the sentence with the missing word.

I _____ my mom every day.

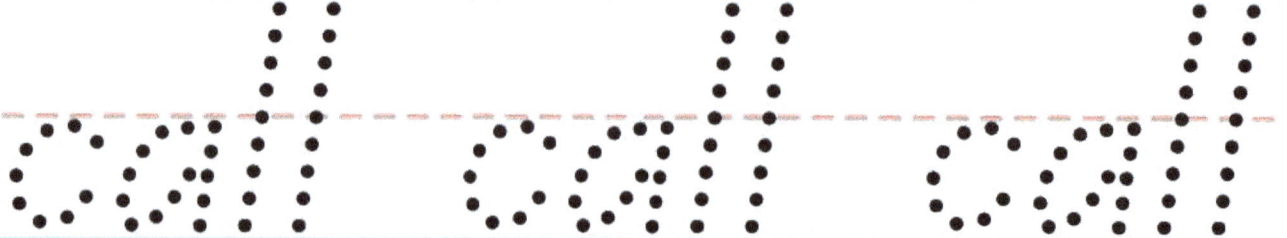

could

- Say the word. Then trace the word.

  could   could

- Write the word.

- Color each space that has the word **could**.

  could   here   green   could

  come   could   she   over

- Complete the sentence with the missing word.

We ___ go home.

LETTER B

Trace the letter **B b**:

Write an upper and lower case letter **B**:

- Color all the items that begin with the **B** sound:

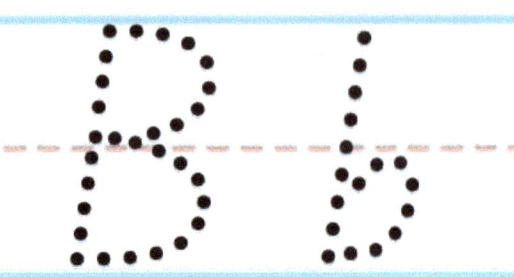

LETTER B

- Say the name of each picture. Draw a line from the letter **B** to each picture that begins with the **b** sound.

LETTER B

• Trace the letter **B b**. Circle the picture in each row whose name begins with the **b** sound.

LETTER B

- Complete the maze. Color the squares that have the letter **B** printed inside.

 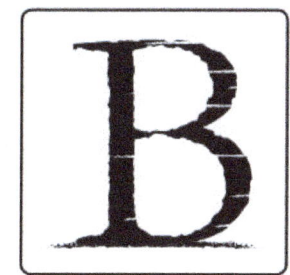 

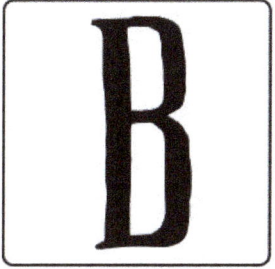  

be

- Say the word. Then trace the word.

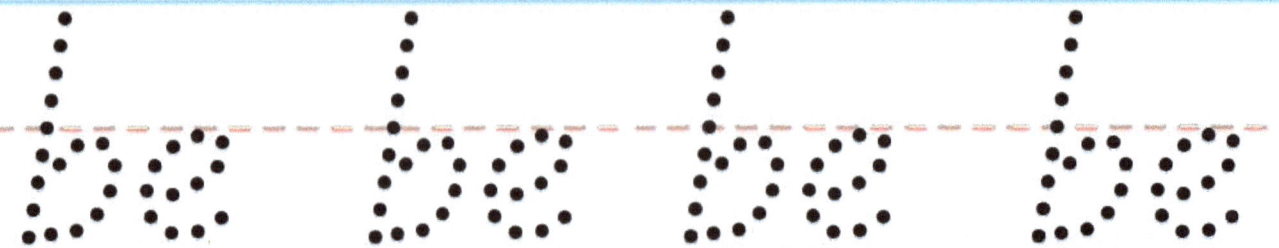

- Write the word.

- Color each space that has the word **be**.

my	be	are	be	out	get
as	find	and	be	see	me
be	more	be	all	day	I

- Complete the sentence with the missing word.

I like to ___ good.

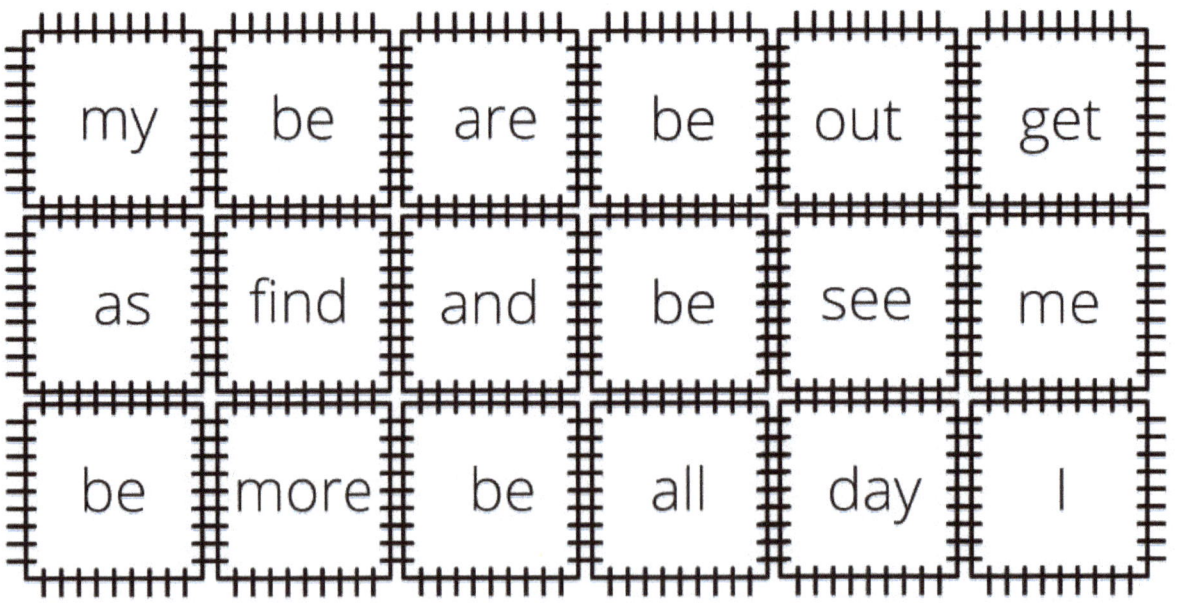

big

- Say the word. Then trace the word.

  big   big   big

- Write the word.

- Fill in the missing letters to write the word.

b__g   bi__

__ig   _i_

b__   __g

- Complete the sentence with the missing word.

I like _____ presents.

before

- Say the word. Then trace the word.

before before

- Write the word.

- Find and circle the word **before** three times.

m d l b e f o r e
o b e f o r e r g
r n a s t r r b a
b e f o r e f m q

- Complete the sentence with the missing word.

I want milk _____ going out .

- Say the word. Then trace the word.

by by by by

- Write the word.

- Circle each apple that has the word **by**.

make • by • my • look • here
by • see • by • you • by

- Complete the sentence with the missing word.

This was made ___ grandma.

LETTER N

Trace the letter **N n**:

Write an upper and lower case letter **N**:

- Color all the items that begin with the letter **N**:

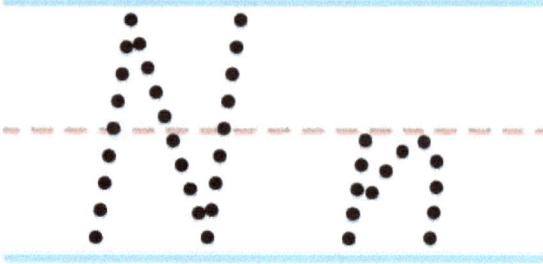

LETTER N

- Trace the letter **N n**. Circle the picture in each row whose name begins with the **n** sound.

LETTER N

- Complete the maze. Color the squares that have the letter **N** printed inside.

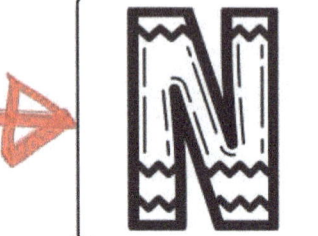  

  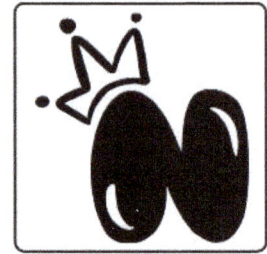

LETTER N

- Say the name of each picture. Draw a line from the letter **N** to each picture that begins with the **n** sound.

no

- Say the word. Then trace the word. Write the word.

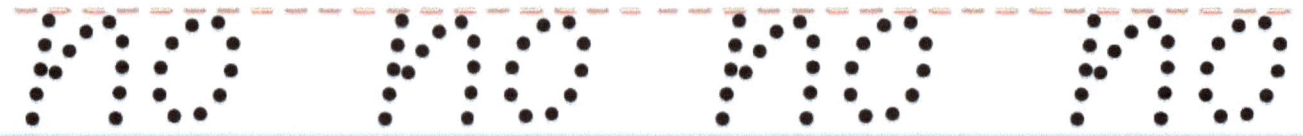

- Color each star that has the word **no**.

- Complete the sentence with the missing word.

I see ___ problem.

now

- Say the word. Then trace the word. Write the word.

  now now now

- Find the word **now**. Draw a line to connect the letters.

  [n] [d] [w] [a]

  [w] [o] [p] [m]

- Complete the sentence with the missing word.

  _____ you see me.

not

- Say the word. Then trace the word. Write the word.

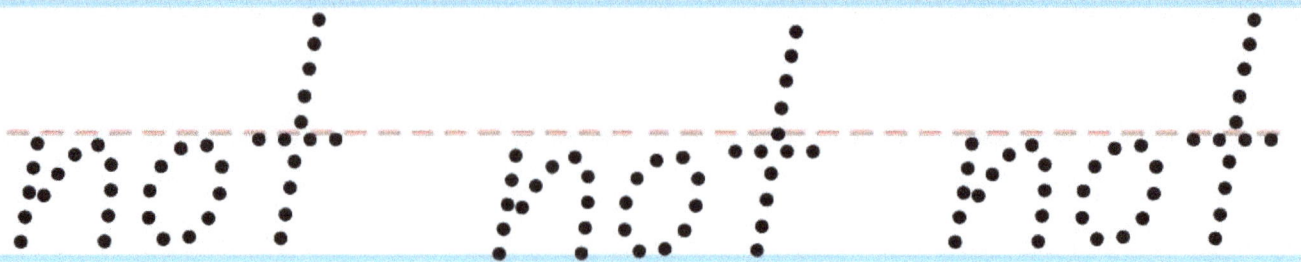

- Fill in the missing letters to write the word.

n_t **_ot** **no_**

_ _t **_o_** **n_ _**

- Complete the sentence with the missing word.

Do _____ enter!

number

- Say the word. Then trace the word. Write the word.

number

- Find and circle the word **number** three times.

n u m b e r o r t
h t h i s o d r h
i n u m b e r b i
s f h n u m b e r

- Complete the sentence with the missing word.

What _____ is this?

LETTER K

Trace the letter **K k**:

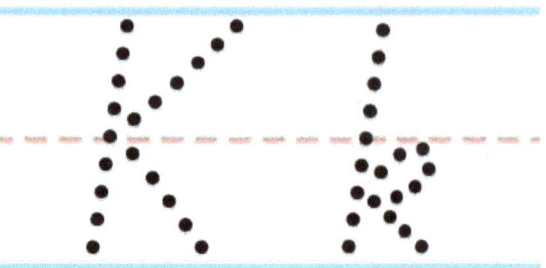

Write an upper and lower case letter **K**:

- Color all the items that begin with the letter **K**:

LETTER K

- Trace the letter **K k**. Circle the picture in each row whose name begins with the **k** sound.

LETTER K

- Say the name of each picture. Draw an **X** on each picture that begins with the **K** sound:

LETTER K

- Trace the letter **K k**. Say the name of each picture. Draw a line from letter **K k** to each picture that begins with the **k** sound.

- Say the name of each picture. Circle the letter of the beginning sound.

- Say the name of each picture. Circle the letter of the beginning sound.

LETTER V

Trace the letter **V v**:

Write an upper and lower case letter **V**:

- Color all the items that begin with the letter **V**:

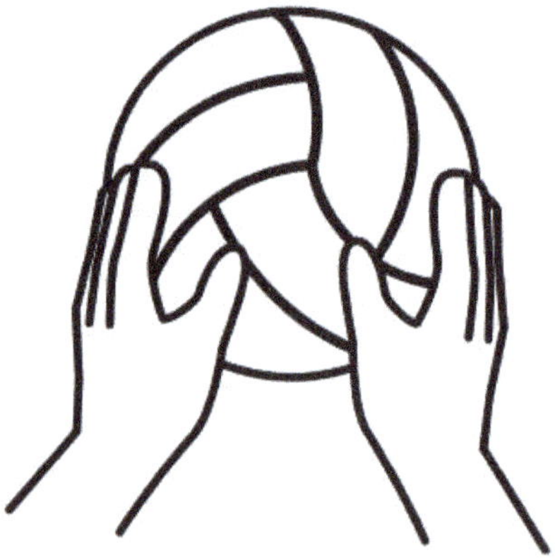

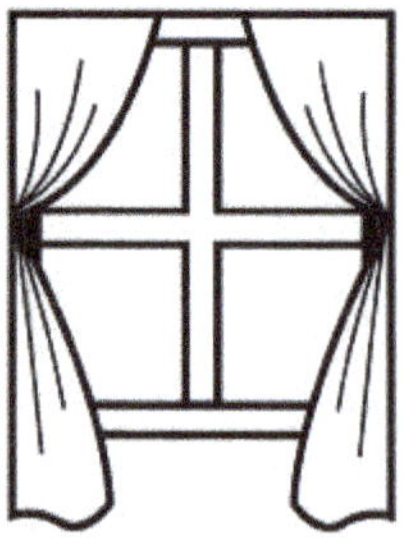

LETTER V

- Trace the letter **V v**. Circle the picture in each row whose name begins with the **v** sound.

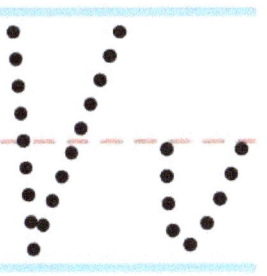   

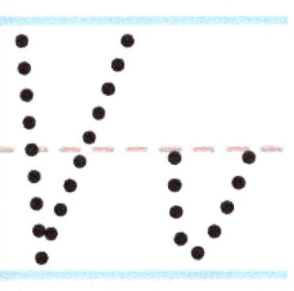   

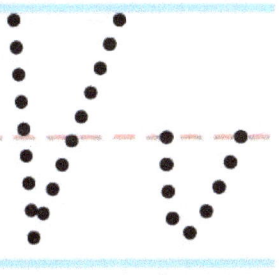   

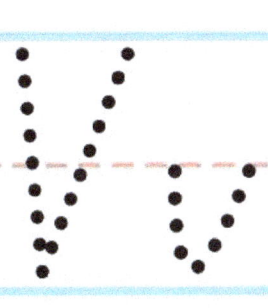   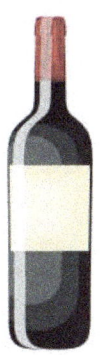

LETTER V

- Say the name of each picture. Draw a line from letter **V** to each picture that begins with the **v** sound.

LETTER V

- Complete the maze. Color the squares that have the letter **V** printed inside.

 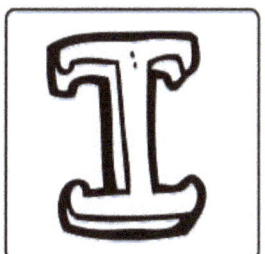 

 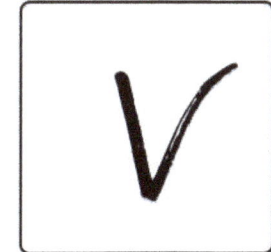 

- Say the name of each picture. Circle the letter of the beginning sound.

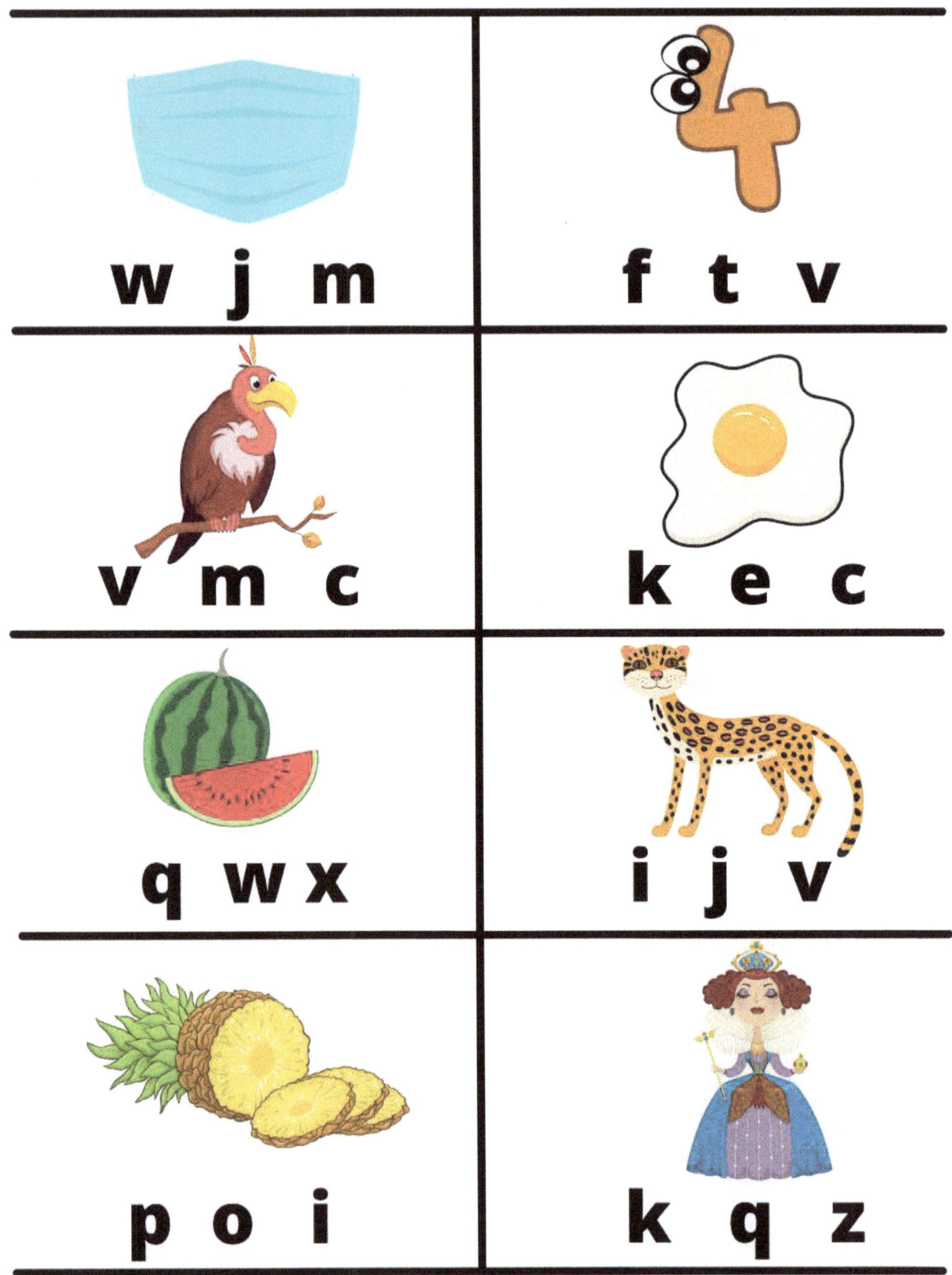

135

- Say the name of each picture. Circle the letter of the beginning sound.

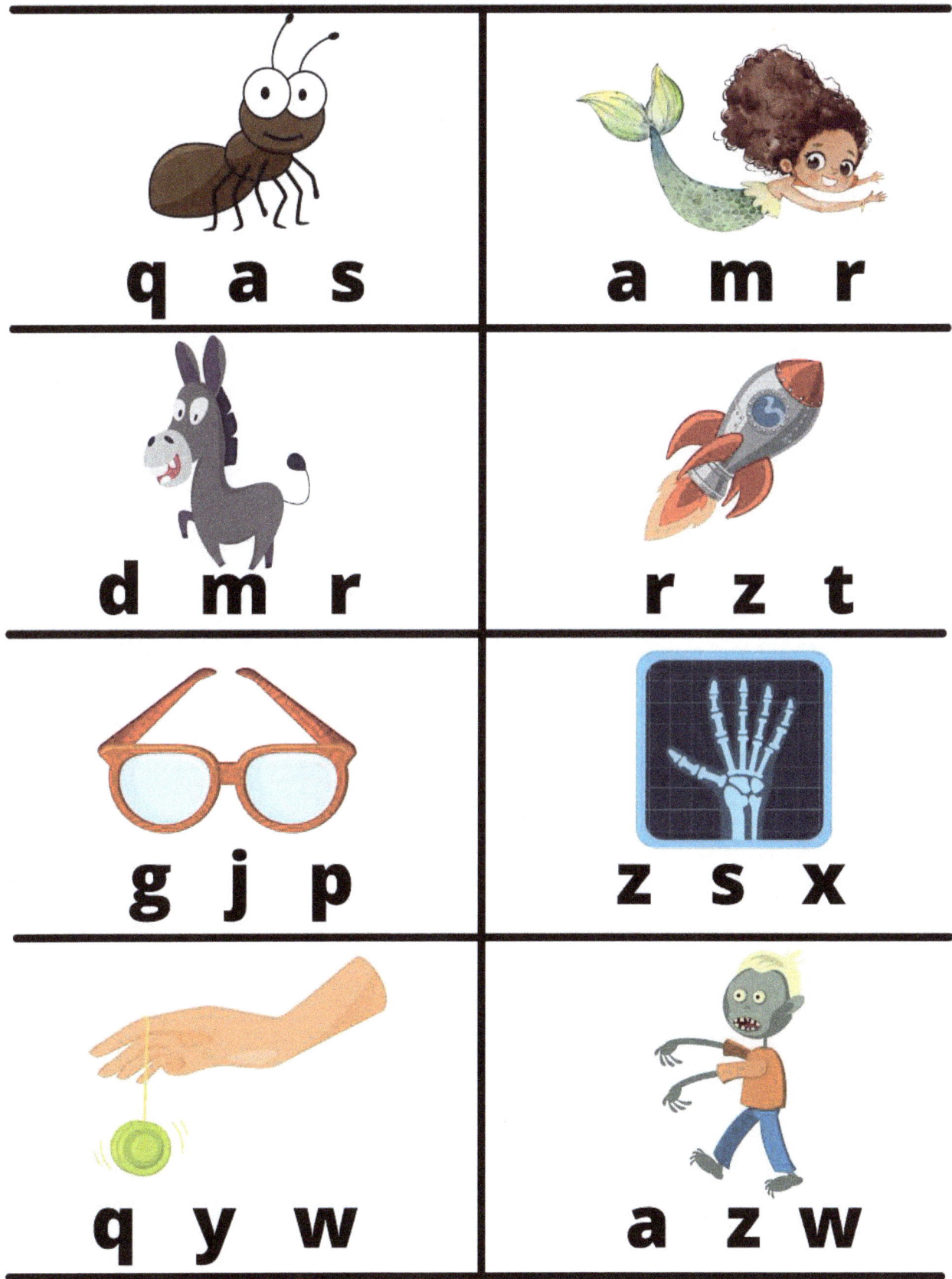

LETTER E

Trace the letter **E e**:

Write an upper and lower case letter **E**:

- Color all the items that begin with the letter **E**:

LETTER E

- Trace the letter **E e**. Circle the picture in each row whose name begins with the **e** sound.

LETTER E

- Say the name of each picture. Circle each picture that begins with the sound **E**:

LETTER E

- Complete the maze. Color the squares that have the letter **E** printed inside.

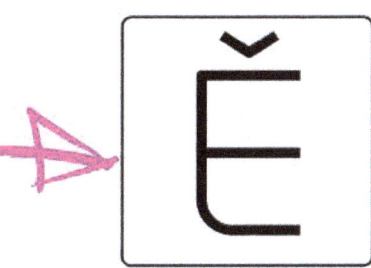  

  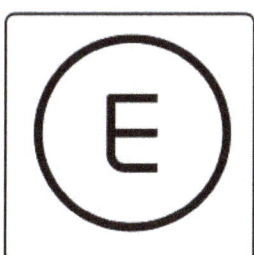

 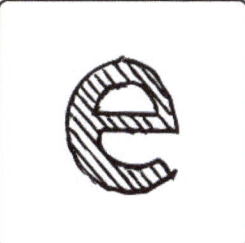 

  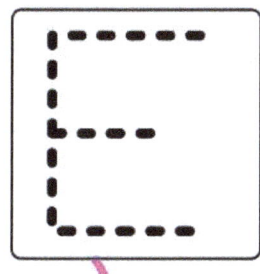

each

- Say the word. Then trace the word. Write the word.

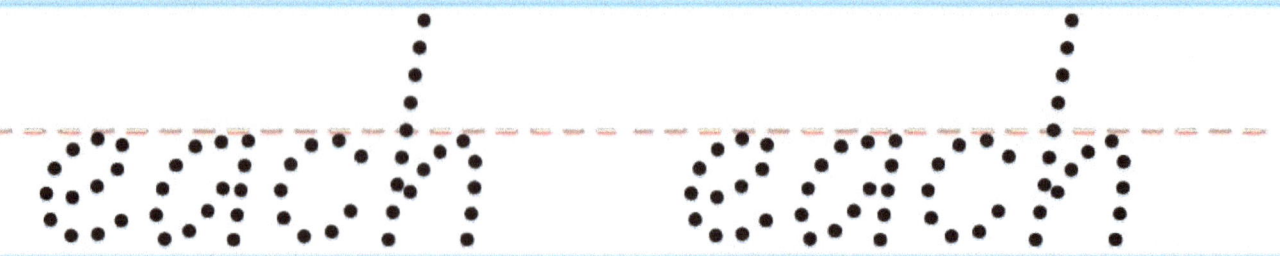

- Color each space that has the word **each**.

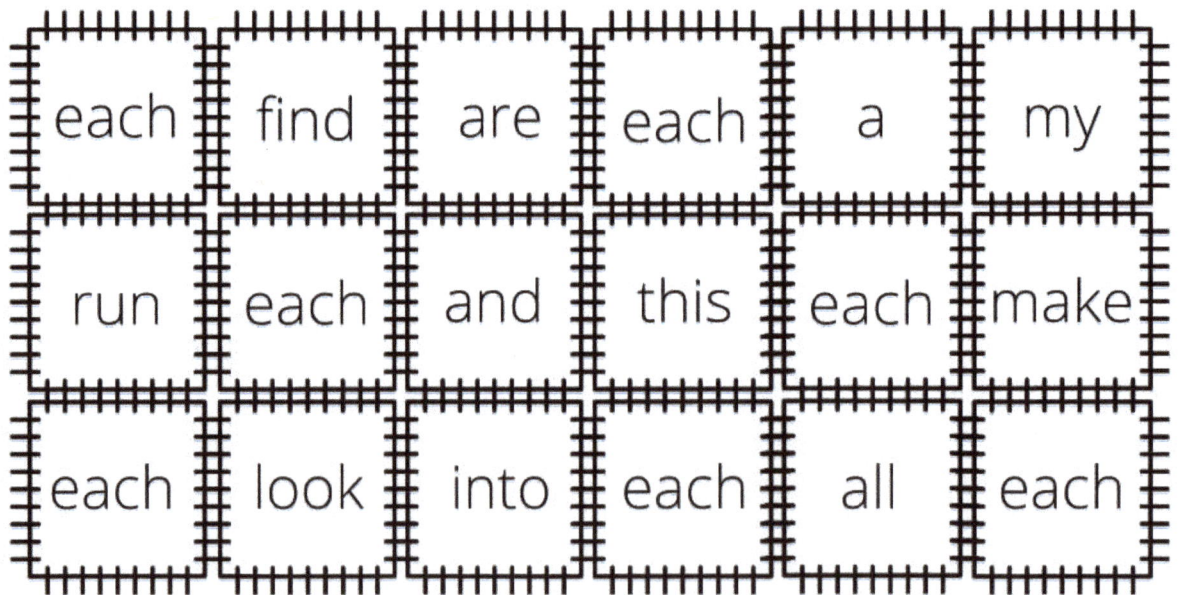

- Complete the sentence with the missing word.

I see _____ letter.

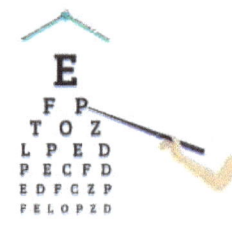

Word search

- Can you find all the sight words in the puzzle bellow?

e	x	b	h	p	f	s	e	e
a	r	e	u	n	r	d	m	e
c	s	z	l	q	o	n	a	y
h	a	v	e	u	m	a	m	i
m	z	l	f	o	c	o	m	e
r	u	n	l	u	i	d	a	y
c	d	z	b	q	o	h	g	z
m	o	r	e	f	s	h	e	f

Word Search

each	day
are	she
more	run
from	have
see	come

LETTER W

Trace the letter **W w**:

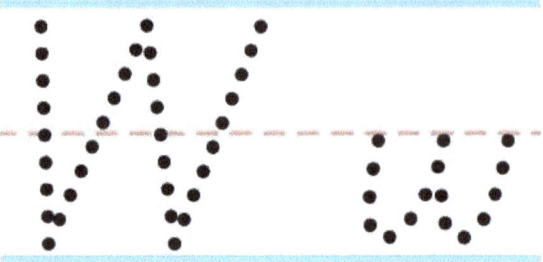

Write an upper and lower case letter **W**:

- Color all the items that begin with the **W** sound:

LETTER W

- Say the name of each picture. Circle each picture that begins with the **w** sound.

LETTER W

- Color only the squares with letter **W**.

LETTER W

- Say the name of each picture. If it begins with the sound **W**, write **W w** on the line.

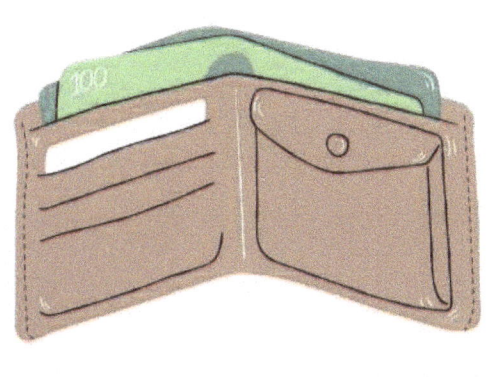

write

- Say the word. Then trace the word.

  write   write

- Write the word.

- Fill in the missing letters to write the word.

wr_te _rite w_ite

_ _ite wri_ _ w_i_e

- Complete the sentence with the missing word.

I love to _____ letters.

- Say the word. Then trace the word.

- Write the word.

- Circle each walnut that has the word **we**.

- Complete the sentence with the missing word.

___ like to write.

was

- Say the word. Then trace the word.

was was was

- Write the word.

- Find and circle the word **was** three times.

a d w a s
s b c x a
s w a s s
c f w a s

- Complete the sentence with the missing word.

Your brother _____ here.

what

- Say the word. Then trace the word.

  what   what

- Write the word.

- Color each space that has the word **what**.

- Complete the sentence with the missing word.

_____ are you doing now?

150

when

- Say the word. Then trace the word.

  when   when

- Write the word.

- Fill in the missing letters to write the word.

  wh_n   _hen   wh_n

  __en   wh__   ___n

- Complete the sentence with the missing word.

  ____ is your birthday?

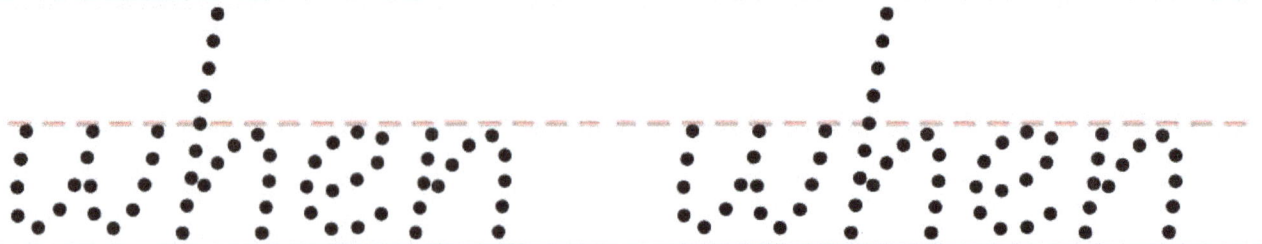

- Say the word. Then trace the word.

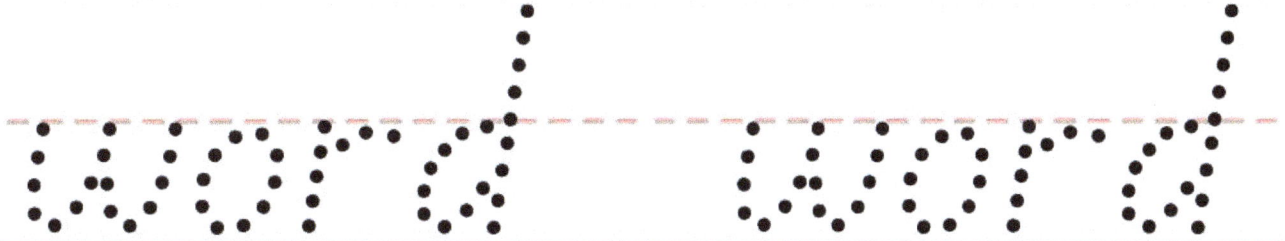

- Write the word.

- Color each space that has the word **word**.

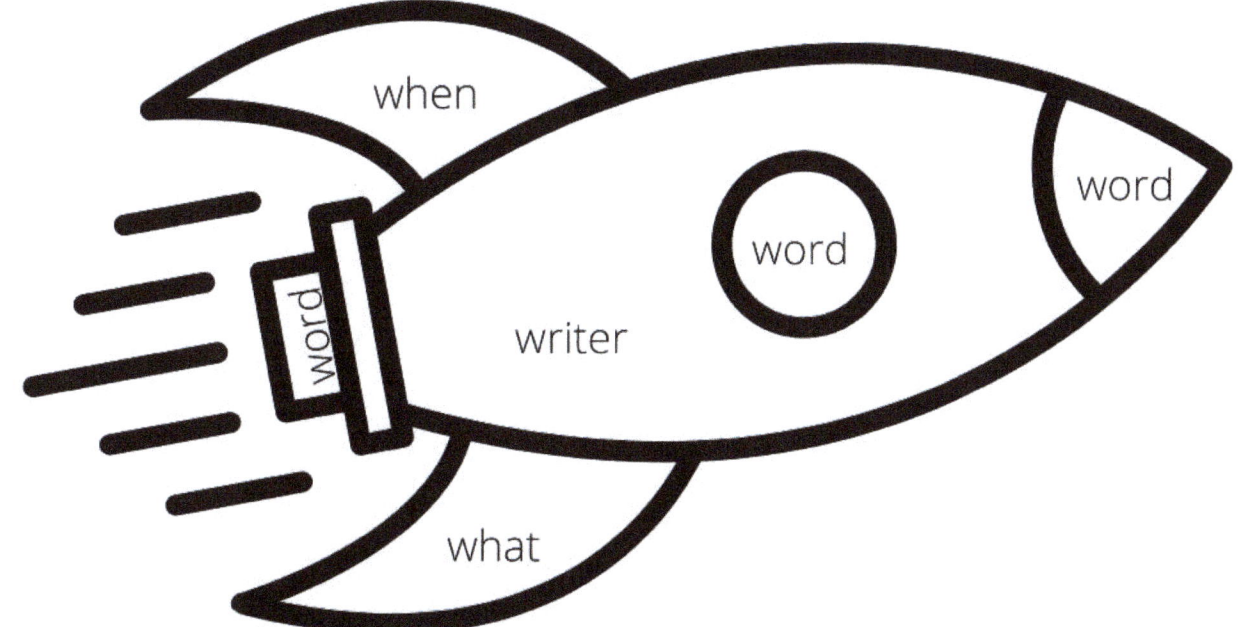

- Complete the sentence with the missing word.

I gave you my ___.

LETTER J

Trace the letter **J j**:

Write an upper and lower case letter **J**:

- Color all the items that begin with the **J** sound:

LETTER J

- Say the name of each picture. Draw a line from the letter **J** to each picture that begins with the **j** sound.

LETTER J

- Trace the letter **J j**. Circle the picture in each row whose name begins with the **j** sound.

155

LETTER J

- Complete the maze. Color the squares that have the letter **J** printed inside.

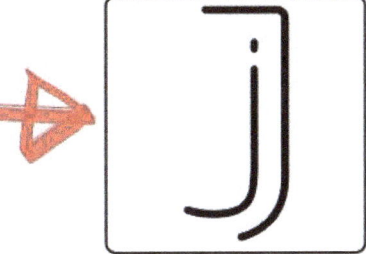  

  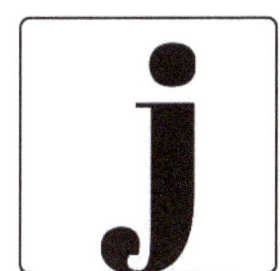

 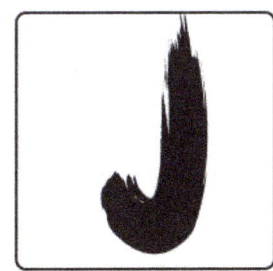 

 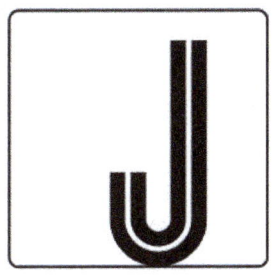 

just

- Say the word. Then trace the word.

just just just

- Write the word.

- Fill in the missing letters to write the word.

j_st   jus_

_ust

ju_ _   _ _st

- Complete the sentence with the missing word.

I ____ had breakfast.

short a

- Circle the word in each box that has the **short a** sound, as in **cap**.

mac / map / mop	tag / tug / tip
him / hen / ham	mask / mist / more
can / cob / car	him / hat / hot
big / bag / bug	beg / bug / bat

LETTER P

Trace the letter **P p**:

Write an upper and lower case letter **P**:

- Color all the items that begin with the letter **P**:

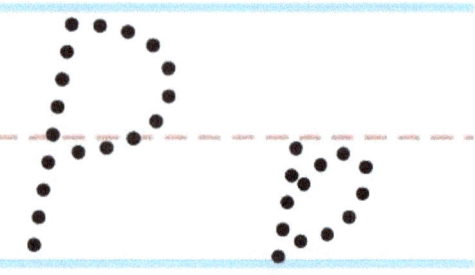

LETTER P

- Trace the letter **P p**. Circle the picture in each row whose name begins with the **p** sound.

LETTER P

- Complete the maze. Color the squares that have the letter **P** printed inside.

  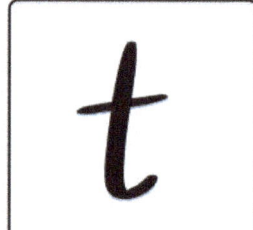

LETTER P

- Say the name of each picture. Draw a line from the letter **P** to each picture that begins with the **P** sound.

short e

- Say the name of each picture. Write the letter **e** to complete each **short e** word.

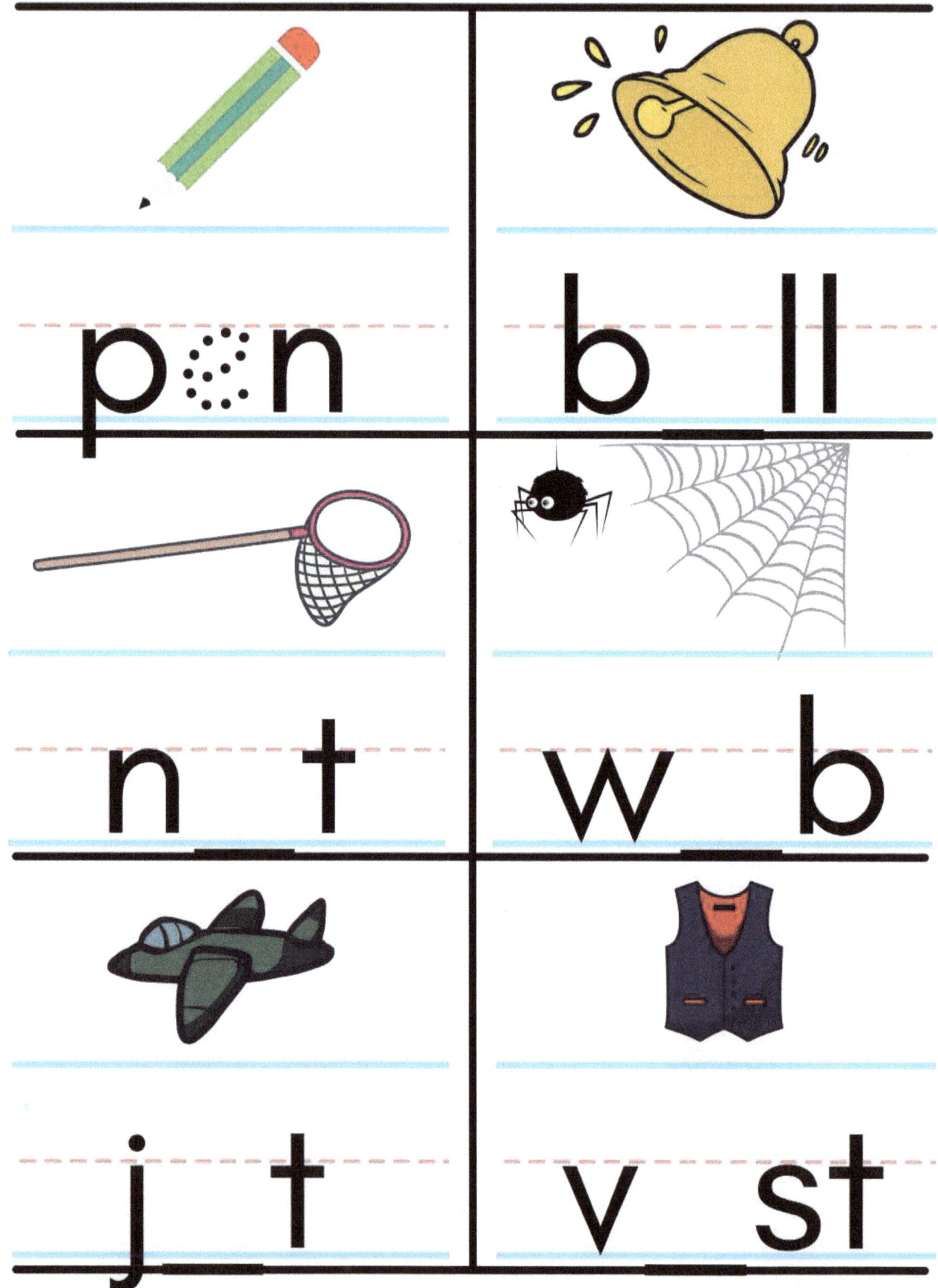

short e

- Circle the word in each box that has the **short e** sound, as in **leg**.

lag / lap / leg	pig / pen / pin
ton / ten / tint	dress / drain / duck
not / nut / net	tent / tip / tint
bag / bell / ball	peg / pan / pin

LETTER Y

Trace the letter **Y** y:

Write an upper and lower case letter **Y**:

• Color all the items that begin with the letter **Y**:

LETTER Y

- Trace the letter **Y y**. Circle the picture in each row whose name begins with the **y** sound.

LETTER Y

- Say the name of each picture. Draw an **X** on each picture that begins with the **Y** sound:

LETTER Y

- Trace the letter **Y y**. Say the name of each picture. Draw a line from letter **Y y** to each picture that begins with the **y** sound.

yes

- Say the word. Then trace the word. Write the word.

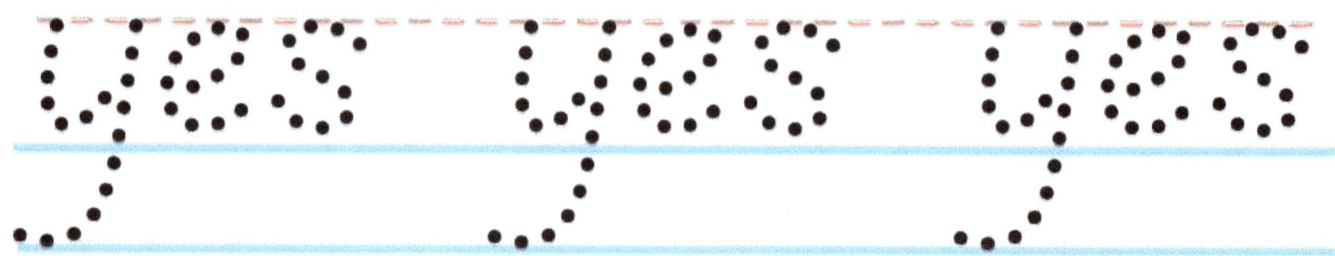

- Color each space that has the word **yes**.

- Complete the sentence with the missing word.

She said _____!

you

- Say the word. Then trace the word. Write the word.

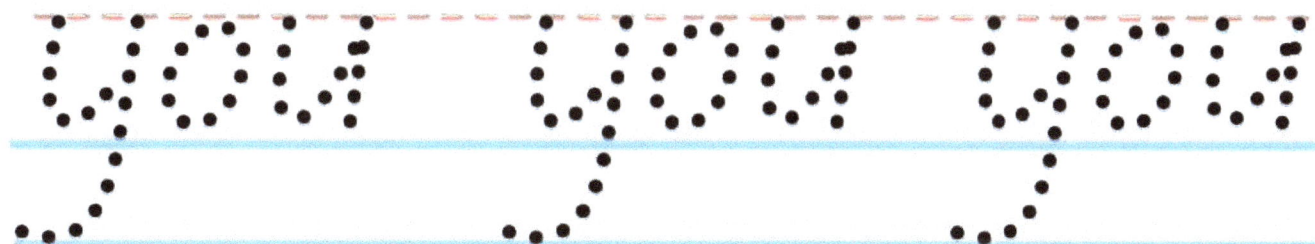

- Find the word **you**. Draw a line to connect the letters.

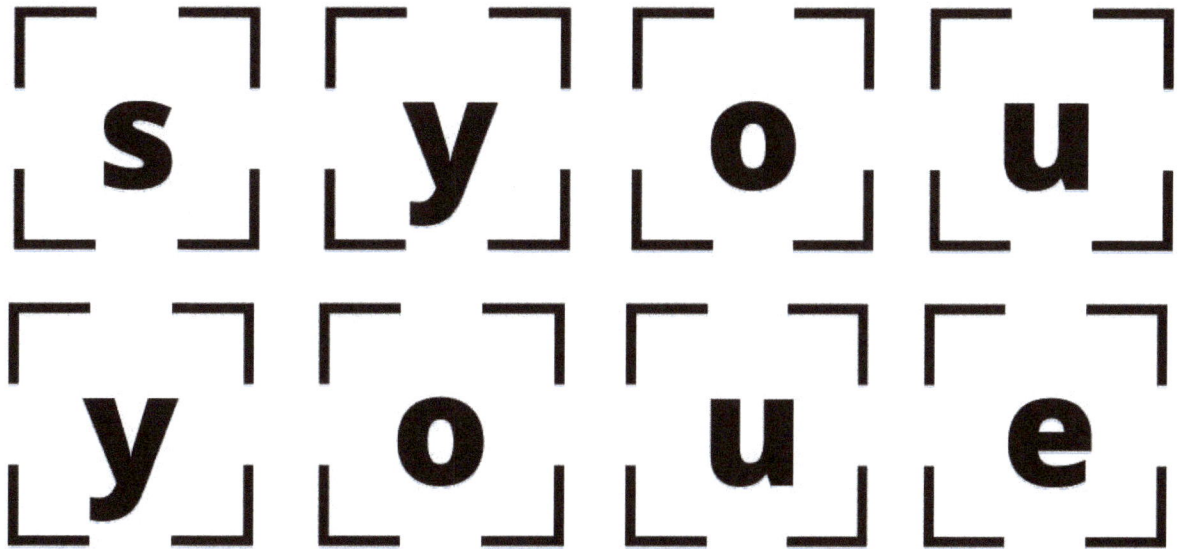

- Complete the sentence with the missing word.

____ **are my best friend.**

yellow

- Say the word. Then trace the word. Write the word.

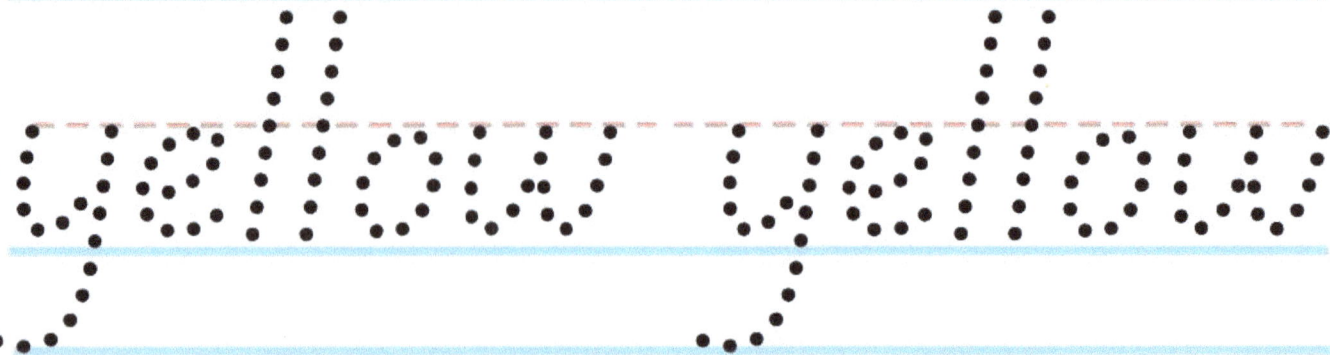

- Circle each fish that has the word **yellow**.

- Complete the sentence with the missing word.

My favorite color is _____.

your

- Say the word. Then trace the word. Write the word.

  your   your

- Fill in the missing letters to write the word **some**.

  you_   _our

  yo_r   y_ _r

  _o_r   y_ _ _

- Complete the sentence with the missing word.

  I like _____ shoes.

LETTER X

Trace the letter **X x**:

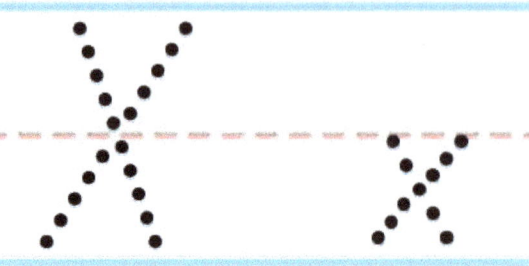

Write an upper and lower case letter **X**:

- Color all the items that begin with the letter **X**:

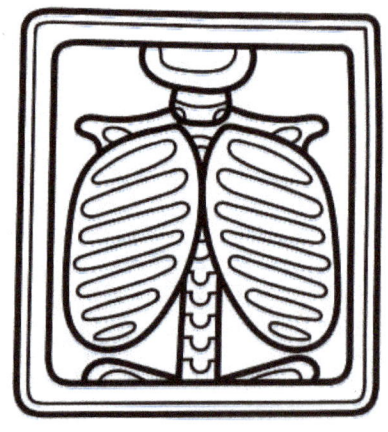

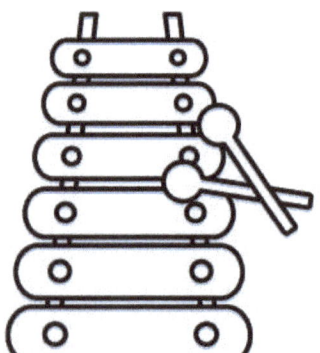

LETTER X

- Complete the maze. Color the squares that have the letter **X** printed inside.

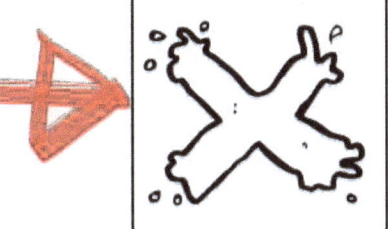  

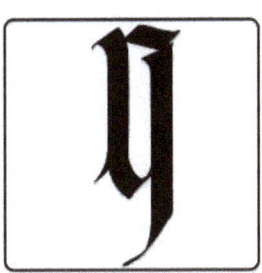  

short *i*

- Say the name of each picture. Write the letter **i** to complete each **short i** word.

f_sh   d_sh

s_x   b_b

p_n_h   k_ng

short *i*

- Circle the word in each box that has the **short i** sound, as in **fig**.

sunk / sand / sink	wig / was / wash
sax / six / sand	fun / fan / fish
log / lips / luck	went / was / wings
bib / bell / ball	peg / pan / pin

LETTER Q

Trace the letter **Q q**:

Write an upper and lower case letter **Q**:

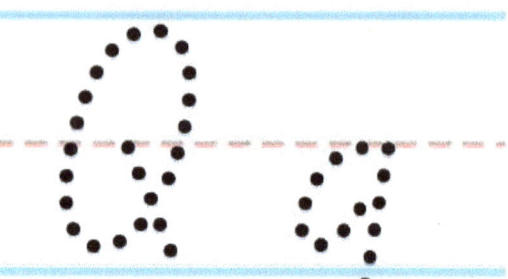

- Color all the items that begin with the letter **Q**:

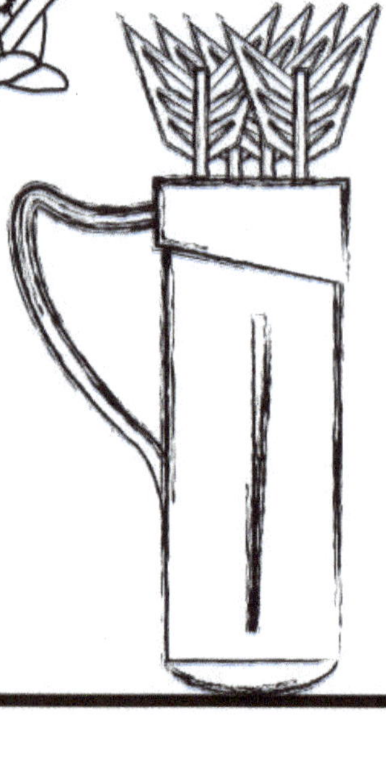

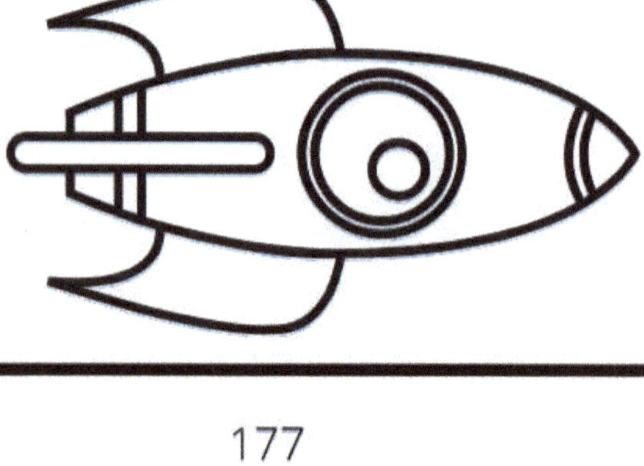

LETTER Q

- Trace the letter **Q q**. Circle the picture in each row whose name begins with the **q** sound.

LETTER Q

- Say the name of each picture. Circle each picture that begins with the sound **Q**:

LETTER Q

- Complete the maze. Color the squares that have the letter **Q** printed inside.

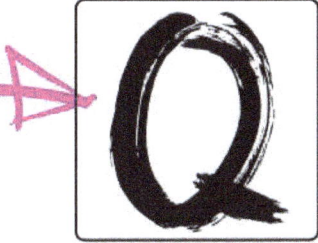  

short o

- Say the name of each picture. Write the letter **o** to complete each **short o** word.

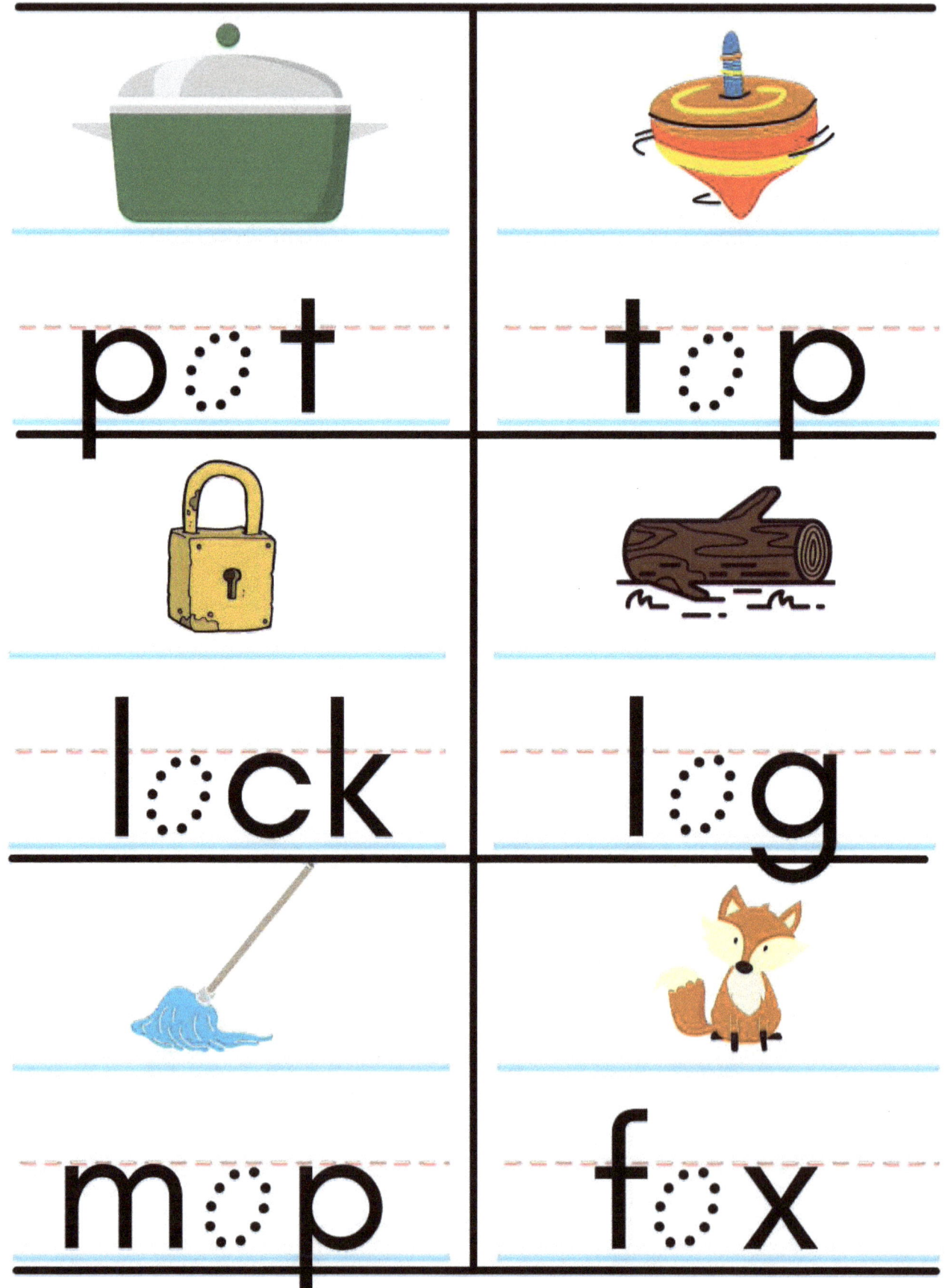

short o

- Circle the word in each box that has the **short o** sound, as in **lock**.

log / lap / leg	dig / dog / den
tap / ten / top	doll / drain / duck
list / lock / lips	sock / sick / sack
fig / frost / frog	peg / pat / pot

LETTER Z

Trace the letter **Z z**:

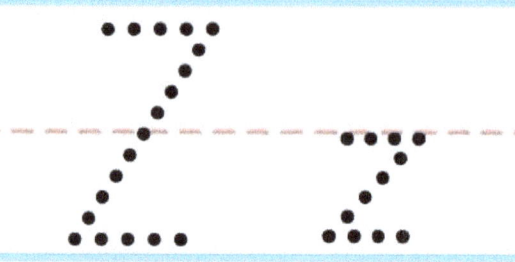

Write an upper and lower case letter **Z**:

- Color all the items that begin with the **Z** sound:

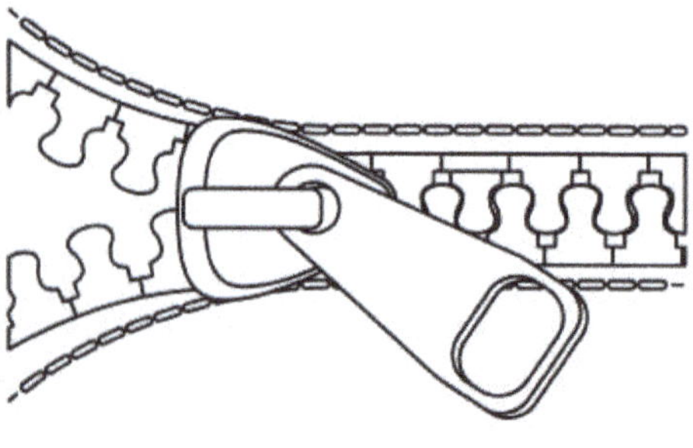

LETTER Z

- Say the name of each picture. Circle each picture that begins with the **Z** sound.

LETTER Z

- Say the name of each picture. Trace the letter **Z** to complete each word.

zero

zoo

zebra

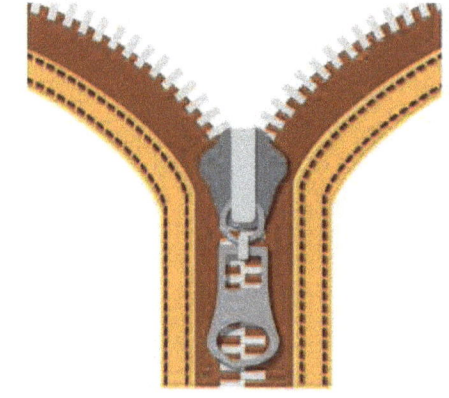

zipper

LETTER Z

- Say the name of each picture. If it begins with the sound **Z**, write **Z z** on the line.

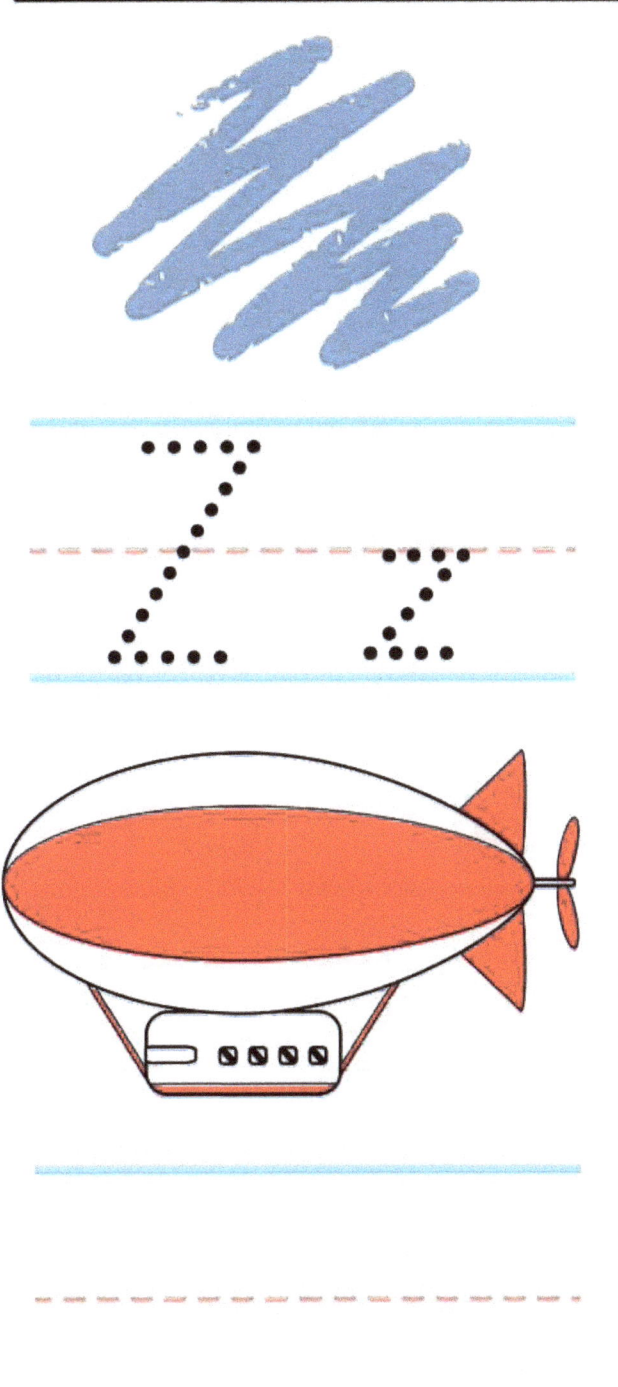

short *u*

- **Say the name of each picture. Write the letter u to complete each short u word.**

short u

- Circle the word in each box that has the **short u** sound, as in **cup**.

mug
man
milk

rot
rug
ray

gap
gum
gas

doll
drain
duck

not
net
nut

sun
sick
sack

jug
jar
jet

dog
drum
dot

Answer Key

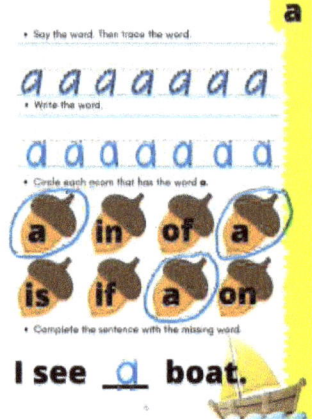

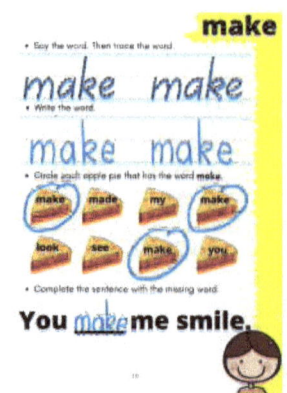

Answer Key

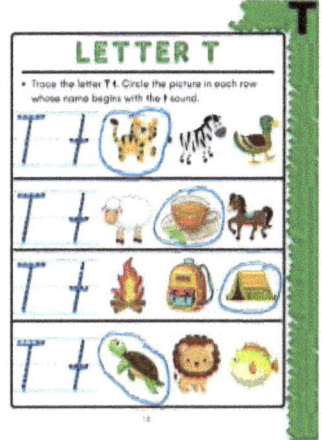

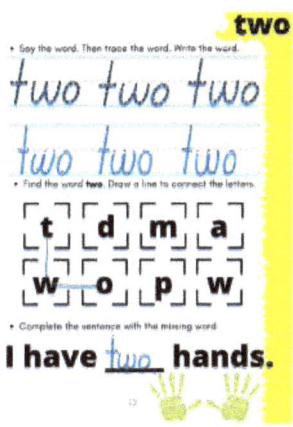
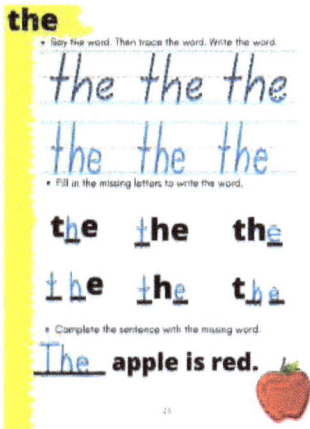

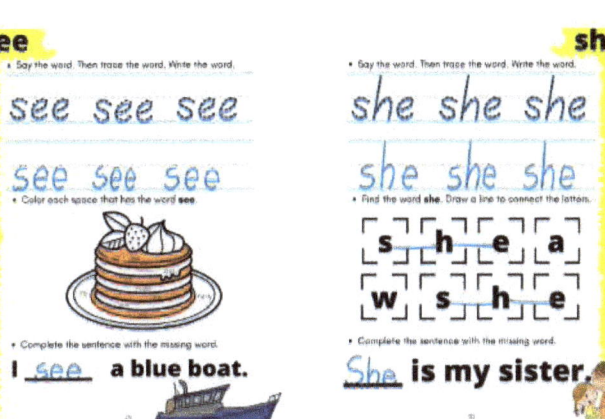

Answer Key

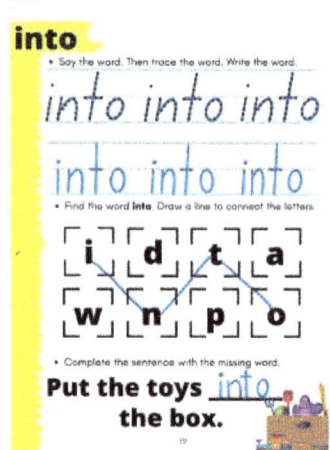

Answer Key

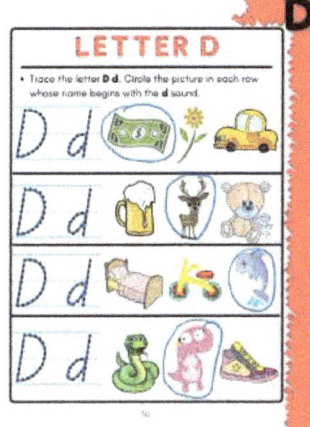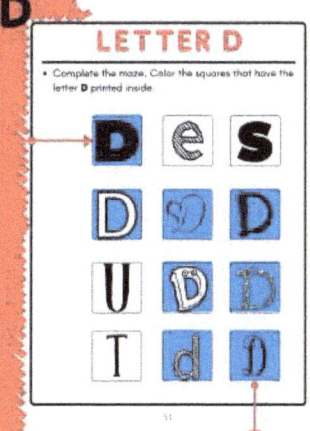
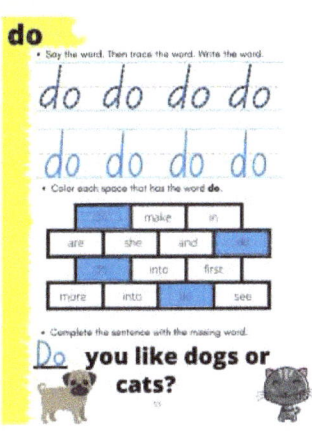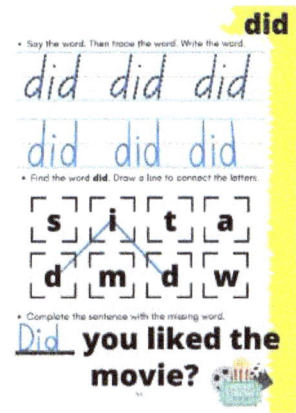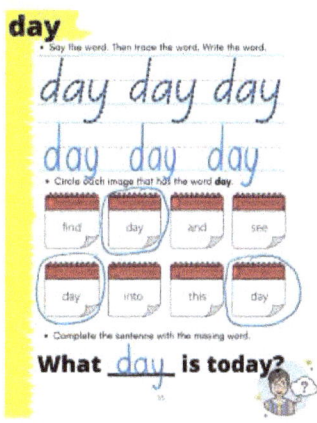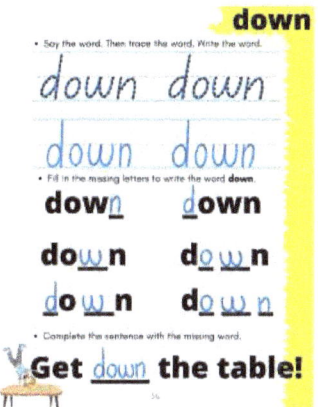

192

Answer Key

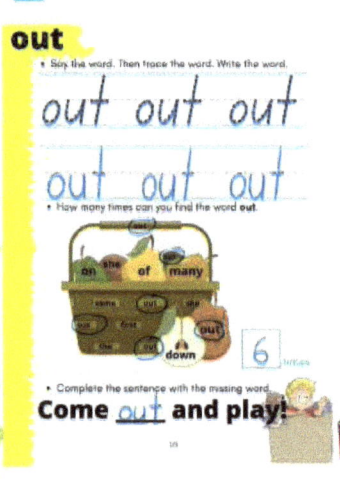
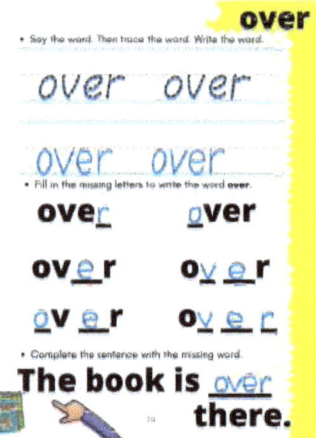

193

Answer Key

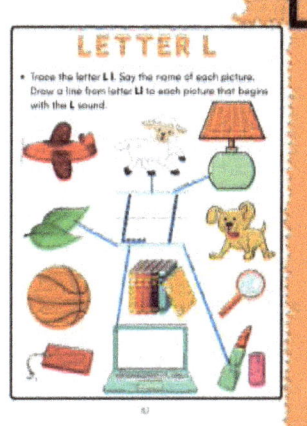

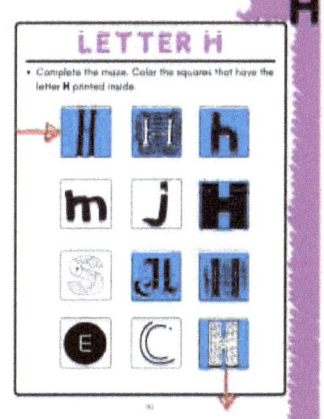

Answer Key

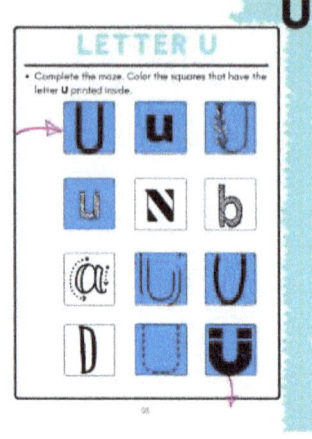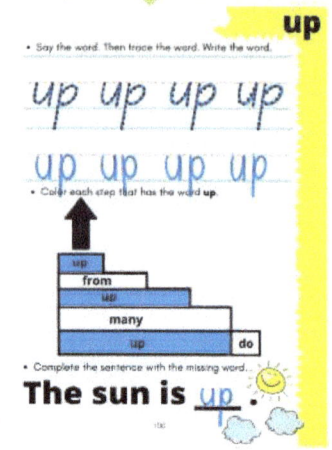

Answer Key

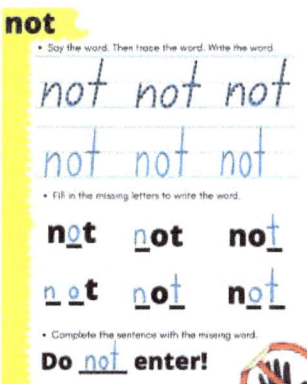
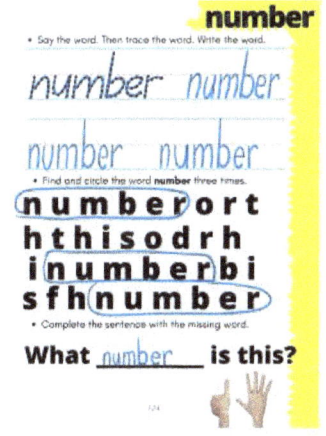

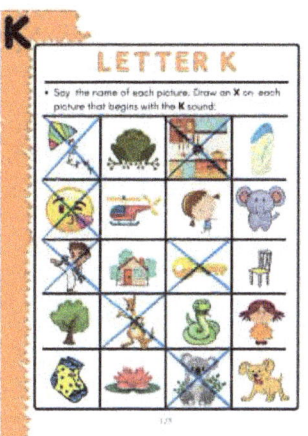

Answer Key

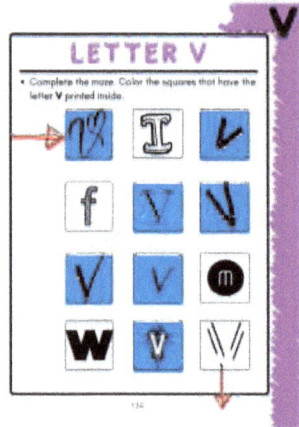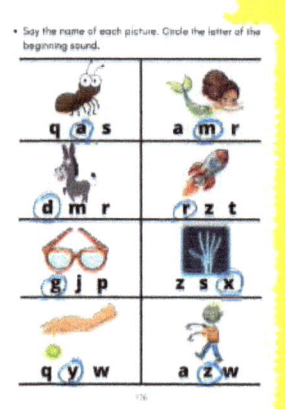
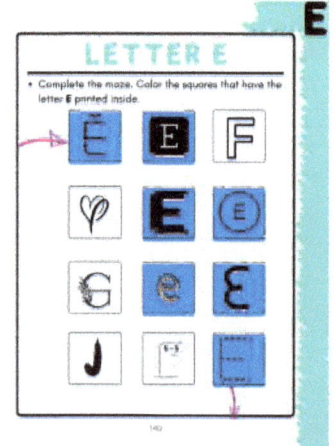

Answer Key

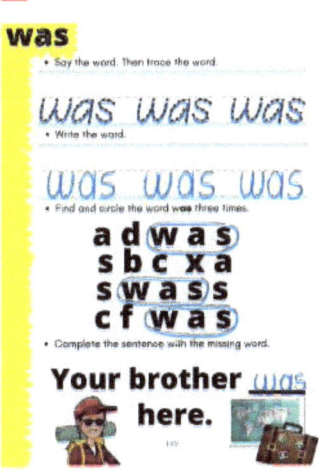

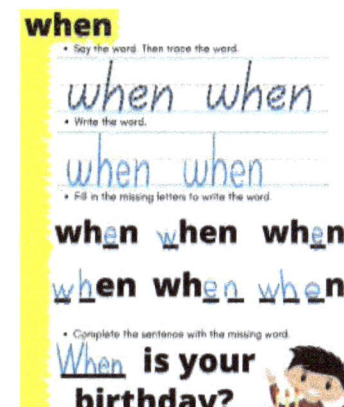

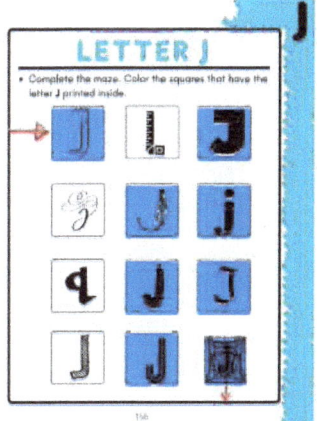

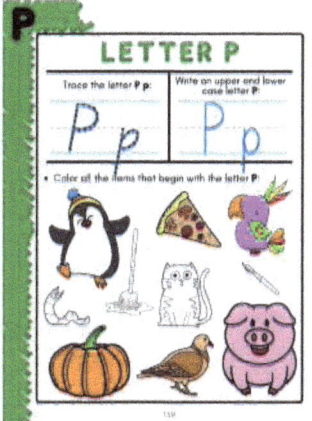

Answer Key

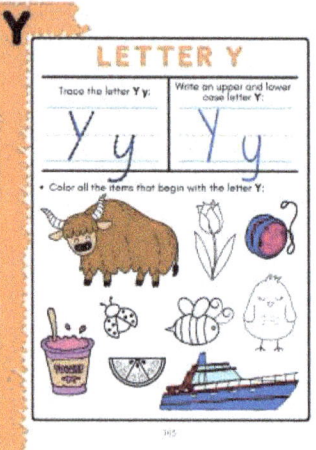   

 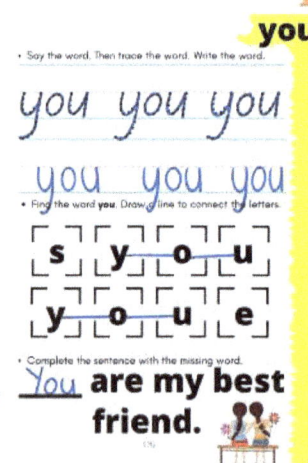  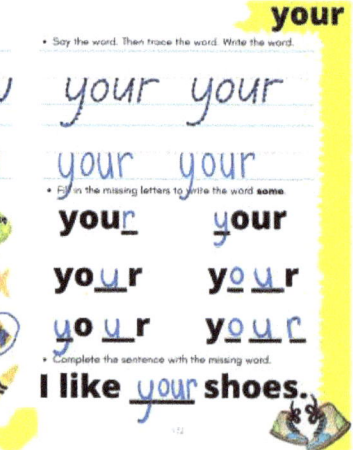

 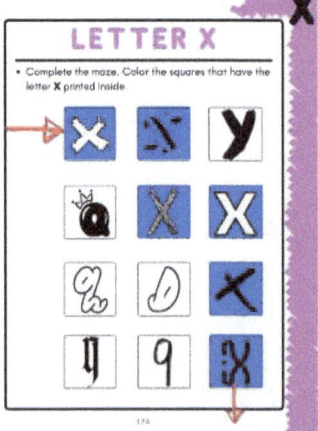  

Answer Key

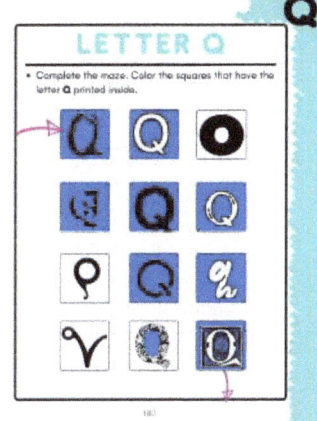
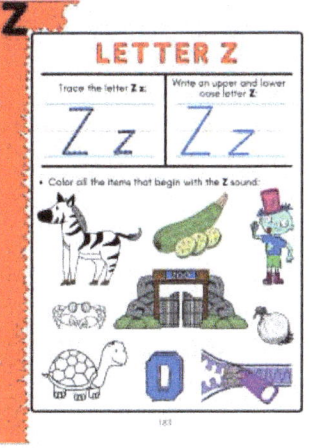

HELLEN M. ANVIL

Join us for a gathering to celebrate a life of continuous learning.

 /helen.anvil

 /helen.anvil

 helen.m.anvil@gmail.com

© **Copyrights 2021 - All rights reserved**

You may not reproduce, duplicate or send the contents of this book without direct written permission from the author. You cannot hereby despite any circumstance blame the publisher or hold him or her te legal responsibility for any reparation, compensation or monetary forfeiture owing to the information included herein, either in a direct or indirect way.

Legal Notice: This book has copyright protection. You can use the book for personal purpose. You should not sell, use, alter, distribute, quote, take excerpts or paraphrase in part of whole the material contained in this book without obtaining the permission of the author first.

Disclaimer Notice: You must take note that the information in this document is for casual reading and entertainment purpose only. We have made every attempt to provide accurate, up to date and reliable information. We do not express or imply guarantees of any kind. The person who read admit that the writer is not occupied in giving legal, financial, medical or other advice. We put this book content by sourcing various places. Please consult a licensed professional before you try any techniques shown in this book. By going through this document, the book lover comes to an agreement that under no situation is the author accountable for any forfeiture, direct or indirect, which they may incur because of the use of material contained in this document, including, but not limited to, - errors, omissions, or inaccuracies.

GREAT JOB!
ACHIVEMENT DIPLOMA

This certifies that

....

has completed all the activities in
Phonics and Sight Words

You are on your way
to becoming a reader!

You are a sight words
superstar!

www.ingramcontent.com/pod-product-compliance
Lightning Source LLC
Chambersburg PA
CBHW061104070526
44579CB00011B/129